INNER
FENG SHUI

For Ven. Roger Kunsang – who planted such profoundly important seeds in my mind. Thank you from my heart.

INNER
FENG SHUI

USING THE ANCIENT CHINESE ART
FOR INNER DEVELOPMENT

LILLIAN TOO

RIDER
LONDON • SYDNEY • AUCKLAND • JOHANNESBURG

First published in 2000

1 3 5 7 9 10 8 6 4 2

Published in 2000 by Rider,
an imprint of Ebury Press, Random House,
20 Vauxhall Bridge Road, London SW1V 2SA
www.randomhouse.co.uk

Random House Australia (Pty) Limited
20 Alfred Street, Milsons Point, Sydney,
New South Wales 2061, Australia

Random House New Zealand Limited
18 Poland Road, Glenfield,
Auckland 10, New Zealand

Random House South Africa (Pty) Limited
Endulini, 5A Jubilee Road, Parktown 2193, South Africa

The Random House Group Limited Reg. No. 954009

Papers used by Rider Books are natural, recyclable products made from wood grown in
sustainable forests.

Printed in Great Britain by Butler & Tanner Ltd, Frome and London

A CIP catalogue record for this book is available from the British Library

ISBN 0 7126 0737 4

Contents

Introduction

Feng shui is an ancient Chinese art and science that teaches us how to live in harmony with the earth. By following its philosophy and methods we can attract good fortune into our lives. Our surroundings – furniture, colour schemes and so on – can be arranged in such a way that the spiritual forces around us work to enhance our lives and ensure that we achieve our highest potential.

Feng shui for the mind means enhancing your life through mental space consciousness. It combines the mind balancing of yin and yang energies on deeper, more spiritual planes of consciousness to bring out all that is best in you, and for you. This inner form of feng shui lifts you to new heights of space and time awareness, gives you a heightened perception that helps to redefine your motivations, clarify all your life's aspirations, and strengthen your resolve to encourage your inner creativity to flow outwards. These developments within your inner space will transform the way you view the world. They will unlock the magnificent inner chi, allowing it to flow outwards and achieve whatever you want at the outer dimensions of your world.

So if you wish to be more successful; if you long for a more interesting job; if you want more money, or better prospects in your career; if you wish you were more confident and could make a quantum leap in improving your performance at school or at work ... If you desire a more interesting personality, and wish you were far more attractive ... if you want to find real love, romance, companionship... Most of all, if you want to create real happiness in your life, you can actualize it by using the methods contained in this book. In fact, if you wish for anything at all, the simple yet powerful techniques for accessing your inner mind can be the key that unlocks a huge store of good fortune and brings it into your life.

Inner feng shui is so powerful simply because the mind is so tremendously powerful – if only you use and engage it consciously. Once you acquire the skill of tapping into its deepest recesses through the proper practice of feng shui techniques, you will be able to arrange your space consciousness to enhance and harmonize your inner rhythms, your flow of energy. Nothing is more powerful than tapping into this inner flow.

The three types of luck

The Chinese believe that we are influenced by three types of luck – heaven, earth and mankind luck. These represent the sum total of the metaphysical influences that determine the quality of our life. First there is the luck which comes from heaven (*tien chai*); secondly there is the luck which comes from the earth (*ti chai)* and thirdly the luck which we create for ourselves (*ren chai*).

- **Heaven luck** determines the circumstances of our birth. We have no control over our heaven luck, but it decides our state in life.
- **Earth luck** is feng shui – the science that offers guidelines on the way we sleep, eat, sit and work, making certain we live in harmonious interface with the landscape and our environment. Feng shui offers specific ways of tapping into the energy lines of the earth, which the Chinese refer to as the dragon's cosmic breath or chi. Harness this good chi, and according to feng shui you are tapping into the luck of the earth. So we have control over earth luck.
- **Mankind luck** is what we create for ourselves through our attitudes, our minds, and the nobility of our actions. The *I Ching* refers to this as the actions and thoughts of the superior man. This is the practice of inner feng shui which uses the mind to access the inner consciousness of our being.

Mankind luck is what this book is about. It requires us to tap into our inner reserves of energy and wisdom to practise what we refer to as inner feng shui. To reach this energy source we use meditation, breathing and visualization. The human breath, like that of the environment, is also called chi, except that in relation to the human body, chi means literally internal breath, or internal strength. Practitioners of Chinese kung fu work strenuously at raising their chi, mostly through mind breath control and meditation. Ancient kung fu experts or monks who are renowned for their martial arts skills are real *si-fus* (masters) at breath control. These masters have such total control over their mind and body that they are able to perform stunning feats that defy the laws of gravity. The powerful chi of your inner, deeper spiritual self allows you to take control of your mankind luck. The more developed this control is, the more effectively you will be able to use your consciousness to attract every type of good fortune into your life.

The inner level of mental consciousness

The inner consciousness of the mind is invisible. It does not reside in the brain. It has no tangible existence. The Buddhists describe it as Emptiness. Others say this consciousness is focused somewhere in the vicinity of your heart chakra – the source of all feelings.

It is at this level of mental consciousness that feng shui practice for the mind begins in a defensive way. This is where to look for the *secret poison arrows* that cause you bad luck, create problems, and make all the things in your life go wrong. They cause unhappiness and immense problems. These arrows make you suffer from incredible bad luck. It is vital that you put all the antidotes in place to overcome, dissolve, block and deflect them.

The secret poison arrows of your inner consciousness are very different from those of your outside physical environment. Inner feng shui operates in a different realm and a different dimension, so the poison arrows here are best described as abstract projections of destructive negative feelings. I categorize these poisons broadly under three types of negative – **Anger**, **Attachment** and **Ignorance** – and deal with them fully in Chapter 3. If you think about it very seriously you will realize that collectively, or each on its own, these three poisons represent the root causes of all of your sufferings, all your unhappiness and all your ill fortune. They must be annihilated if you are to emerge happy, strong and successful. Overcoming these poisons will require you to undertake what I call mental space clearing! You can then start to energize for all the good things that you want.

The tools of feng shui for the mind

With the tools of feng shui for the mind you can undertake powerful inner programming exercises that address the eight aspirations of the inner mental Pa Kua. The Pa Kua, an eight-sided shape, is surrounded by the eight trigrams that form the root of the *I Ching*'s 64 hexagrams. The positioning of the trigrams is the essence of feng shui. The tools of this practice will work towards the following goals:

- developing intuition or inner awareness;
- developing mental stability using the breath;
- developing mental tranquillity which lets you go with the flow to tap into powerful rivers of golden auspicious chi;
- and finally most important of all – developing spirituality consciousness using powerful visualization methods. Visualization features in almost every type of 'magic' and spiritual practice. It is the most powerful tool of the mind!

This is the exciting promise of this book. The methods contained here synthesize highly complex with very simple techniques that have been around for thousands of years. A number of these techniques are also part of esoteric methods contained in different traditional and cultural practices.

I was taught many of these methods separately by wonderfully learned teachers and spiritual masters. For years I used them independently of each other, meditating deep and long on questions that buzzed through my mind. These questions explored the connections between my various meditation practices and my practice of feng shui. I also sought answers to many other manifestations of mystical and metaphysical practices, and in the end I discovered all the answers were already inside me. I only needed practice at unlocking them. It is obvious from the New Age consciousness that is presently sweeping the world that this is something that many others are also discovering.

In recent years I have come to see a pattern emerging. I realize now that my practice of inner space consciousness has brought stunning potency to my practice of feng shui. Indeed feng shui has opened many new doors for me. I see this development as both positive and exhilarating for it creates new horizons for me to explore further. How I react to these opportunities reflects my own aspirations.

When the same happens to you, you too can choose from among the new avenues that open up for you. These can be opportunities at any level of consciousness. They can be totally material, involving the pursuit of riches and wealth; and here let me say that wanting to be rich, powerful and successful is perfectly fine. There is nothing negative in that. For years this was what I pursued. I used feng shui to become rich and successful.

But with the passage of time, my needs grew more complex. I also needed to look after my health and my body. This too I enjoyed by arranging the feng shui of my house in such a way that I kept all the illness stars at bay. So my family and myself have enjoyed a pretty healthy life so far… In the past ten years the latent need for spirituality inside me has become more insistent in looking for answers. I have always had a huge yearning to understand the spiritual consciousness within me. And so after using feng shui to bring myself a very comfortable lifestyle and a healthy body, I turned to feng shui to bring me spiritual happiness as well.

The result of my practice of feng shui to engage the inner reaches of my mind was simply amazing, and I want to share it with you. This is what I consider the actual physical manifestation of the greatest good fortune in my life.

Two years ago I met one of the most amazing beings of our time, the most venerable Lama Zopa Rinpoche. I had always visualized strongly to find a true teacher, someone completely qualified to tell me about the real meaning of life, someone who would inspire me and could show me how to attain the state of permanent happiness. A long time ago I came to realize that wealth and health, while important, would not bring ultimate true happiness. So I wished for a guardian angel, I wished for a God presence. I had read about Tibetan Buddhist high lamas whose practice of spiritual meditation and yoga reached such high levels that they could perform feats of what we think of as physical 'magic' – making things appear and disappear, reading minds, foretelling outcomes of events – but I never thought they really existed in the world.

I never imagined that I would one day find a being like that, a being so spiritual, who comes from a world so alien from mine, yet one with whom I would feel such instant affinity. Rinpoche takes on the shape and form of a very humble monk from the high mountains of the Himalayas. He made contact with me from out of the blue! One day, an hour before my family left for the airport for our holiday a fax came at the precise moment when I was standing by the fax machine. I have to tell you that this is important, because if I had not been there Rinpoche's fax would have been lost among a pile of paper. I would have missed it when I returned.

Rinpoche was inviting me to Bodhgaya in India to advise on the feng shui of the giant Maitreya Buddha statue which was being planned, yet I had no idea who he was. As I did not feel confident to visit India on my own, I asked Yap Cheng Hai my feng shui master to accompany me. Master Yap confirmed my instinctive conviction that a request from such a high lama could not be ignored. Master Yap is a profound and most compassionate Buddhist who knew about perfect beings like Rinpoche. Master Yap is also my dearest big brother whose advice I revere and respect. When he said GO, we flew to India!

In the two years since then, I have discovered that Lama Zopa Rinpoche is indeed a very high lama, recognized by His Holiness the Dalai Lama as the reincarnation of the Lawado Lama, a holy being from the Solu Khumbu region of the Himalayas. Rinpoche has many thousands of students around the world who all revere and love him.

Lama Zopa Rinpoche has been the source of many good things that have happened to me … meeting him has changed my view of many things. At the mundane level, I gave up smoking (after over twenty years trying to do so). I complain less. I appreciate my life a lot more. I have become more positive. I care more for other people. I have become less self-centred. At a more spiritual level, I feel the good in me beginning to flower, slowly and noticeably. And I feel the bad in me starting to fade, also slowly but definitely... More important, I have never felt so happy in my whole life.

So yes, let the practice of feng shui bring you wealth, prosperity and good health on the material plane. Let it satisfy all your lower chakras – the energy points that ensure the satisfaction of your body's physical senses. Let feng shui bring you all the success, all the money, all the relationships that satisfy your sense needs. Having your material needs satisfied makes for a more comfortable life. But don't stop there. Go further...

Let the practice of inner feng shui bring you to higher levels of happiness, the peerless happiness that engages your upper *spiritual* chakras – your heart, your head and your mind. Inner space consciousness – the feng shui of the mind – can create spiritual magic in your life, often in ways you don't at first recognize or realize. It has happened for me. Your own experience may well be completely different: we all have different karma, different destinies. But whatever it brings you is sure to be so achingly beautiful that it will transform your life and perceptions for ever. It has done that for me ... and I pray fervently that it will do the same for you. Inner feng shui can bring you fulfilment and the greatest happiness.

Part 1

1.

Unlocking the awesome potential of your mind

Unlock the awesome potential,
From deep within your Mind

Enhance your life
With inner space consciousness

Set new sights for yourself
Redefine your aspirations
And start learning
All the ways
You can reach the
Highest dimensions of your mind

An enormous capability lies within

Feng shui for the mind uses the brain to tap into your inner space consciousness. Your brain is the physical manifestation of your mind. It is like a sleeping giant – colossal and awesome in its potential. This potential lies dormant within you, inactive and quiescent, waiting to be used. If you want to practise inner feng shui you must learn to tap into the brain's huge capability. When you start to do so, the extent of this capability will astound you.

You will discover things about your brain that will literally blow your mind! You will discover that, like almost everyone else on this earth, you are at present using less than 1 per cent of your brain. This is what scientists have discovered: it is an accepted fact. It is not conjecture or opinion.

The human brain is awesome in all the things it does, as well as in all the things it can probably do. Only a tiny handful of individuals possess the secret of unlocking the brain's full potential.

Your mind is the source from which the brain gets its signals. Controlling the mind is what inner feng shui attempts to do. Your brain receives and works on the impulses, signals, energy or chi which your mind conveys to the brain … so this whole process can be seen as a flow of energy, a flow of chi sent from deep within you to manifest itself on the physical plane of your existence. Signals are sent to every part of the physical body, activating and energizing, galvanizing it into action, flooding it with feelings that can be either positive or negative.

Through these signals a flow of inner chi is created which can be auspicious or inauspicious. When these signals are positive and auspicious, they arouse you into acquiring and developing skills, talents, strengths and capabilities way beyond your present expectations. They propel you to attain heights of success, make the kind of income, sustain the kind of relationships and successfully create the lifestyle that will bring you real happiness and satisfaction. Positive stimulation from the brain originates from deep inside you, and is the most powerful cause of good fortune.

On the other hand, when the signals are negative and inauspicious they cause indolence, intolerance, depression, weakness and a complete absence of motivation. These are the root causes of misfortunes and bad luck.

Feng shui for the mind works by focusing on the real source of all good fortune – the deepest recesses of your mind. But before we do that it is important to understand how the brain works and serves the mind. By knowing *how* your inner auspicious chi is conveyed and translated into all kinds of good fortune on the physical plane, you will become very efficient in mastering this dimension of feng shui practice.

The mysterious depths of the mind

It is only in recent years that research in physics, biochemistry and psychology has been focusing on the mysterious depths of the mind's capabilities – in the process gaining greater understanding of the human brain, the physical boundary of the mind. This description is mine, since even now all assumptions of the brain's connection with the mind are conjecture. No one knows for certain exactly how the mind connects with the brain. The brain is physical, and thus can be scientifically studied. Since the mind is intangible and abstract, we examine the scientific findings of the brain to give us clues into the nature of the mind.

Studies on the human brain reveal that its latent potential is far greater than was ever imagined. Exciting findings concern the intricacies of the brain's 'frontiers' – its different functions and the unique characteristics of its left and right sides. Your brain functions like a supercomputer. It has amazing visual, audio, mathematical, analytical and even psychic abilities and capacities. These are supported by millions of brain cells that connect and interact with each other in ways still not fully known.

What *is* known is that there are no limits to the brain's inventiveness and abilities. Anyone can be as creatively imaginative as they allow themselves to be. Anyone can be as deductive, as analytical, and as instinctive as they wish. The brain sets no limits. The brain works according to instructions received from someone or something. We assume this something to be the mind, *your* mind. We assume that someone to be *you*!

The brain is the 'hardware' that your mind uses to create the attitudes, feelings, perceptions, expectations and end results you desire and wish for. The brain is *your* loyal and obedient servant. Understand this, and you will begin to free yourself of limiting restrictions to the way you assess yourself and your capabilities. To explore the inner space consciousness of your mind, start by learning facts about your brain. This will give you the confidence and the conviction to move further into the inner reaches and realms of your mind.

The mind is completely *empty* with no tangible existence. It is invisible but it is potent. This is because it controls your brain. When you control your mind, you control your brain. It then does exactly what *you* will it to do to bring you success and good fortune.

When you have little or no control over your mind, you have no control over your brain, and hence no control over your physical actions and efforts. You will have little control over your own good or bad fortune. At its worst, your mind controls you, and when this happens all your actions lack direction. Your mind has no focus and little chance of bringing you any kind of good fortune. The mind creates obstacles, blockages and dead ends to your good luck.

The mind then becomes the cause of all your bad luck.

But the mind is also the source of all the good fortune in your life. Understand this and you will have grasped the essence of inner feng shui: you will realize that the attainment of a good life, as well as the achievement of brilliance in your life, is well within your scope. You can have anything you want.

When you are expert in practising feng shui for the mind you have the key to a huge treasure house, you unlock a deluge of great good fortune! This treasure lies within you. And the connection between this inner source of good fortune and your outside physical environment and material reality is the brain. Communication from outside to inside to outside again is via the brain!

Getting to know the brain

As recently as our parents' day, very little was known about the brain or the way it operates. People were 'branded' stupid or clever, artistic or numerate, intellectual or obtuse, when it came to assessing mental abilities.

Formal schooling taught a range of subjects but educators paid scant attention to the brain and its functions.

Few schools in the world taught their students how the brain absorbs, stores or regurgitates information. Schoolchildren learnt nothing (or very little) about brain cells and connective tissues. Rarely were they taught how memory comes about, how the eyes move when taking in information, how learning takes place, how pictures get created in the head, where imagination comes from, how creativity is nourished. Children never really knew which part of the brain they were using, and, more important, how they could use more of the brain.

This was because so little was known about the brain. It is only in this generation that we have come to realize how problems connected with seemingly inadequate mental abilities have less to do with the brain's basic capacity than with genuine ignorance of the brain's formidable potential.

The brain is capable of performing more than adequately even when we place it under tremendous stress. We know it has strength and resilience. It can process a huge amount of knowledge, emotions and attitudes. So we know it must have tremendous storage capacity for information, and probably a super-efficient filing system.

But how does it work? How does it respond to commands and stimulus from us? How does it connect with the mind?

Left and right brains

Actually, we have not one but two brains. We have a left brain and a right brain, like the east and west side of the Pa Kua, or eight-sided shape. We have a daring analytical side and a quietly fierce and protective side, the brave green dragon and the ferocious white tiger. The two brains are biologically identical in structure and they work side by side. The two sides operate best when there is perfect balance and harmony. No one side should dominate. Each of the two brains is made up of millions of brain cells which resemble baby octopuses, complete with flailing arms that reach out and connect with other cells.

The two brains have completely different functions. The left brain controls the right side of the body and the right brain controls the left side of the body. Injury to the left brain thus causes the right side of the body to become paralysed, and vice versa.

Intensive research into left and right brains at the University of California has revealed that each brain also controls different intellectual activities. This research measured brain waves emanating from minds engaged in different activities that ranged from the purely creative and imaginary to the exclusively logical and quantitative. The findings of these experiments are now widely acknowledged – that the two sides to our brains, control different types of mental activity.

The right brain takes care of different dimensions – dreaming, colours, rhythms, music and other thought processes requiring creativity, vivid imagination, originality, inventiveness and artistic flair. Right-brain thinking seemed less bounded by scientific and mathematical perimeters. In feng shui terms *the right brain signifies the mighty dragon* who is courageous and brave, daring to seek out and experiment in areas where other lesser beings fear to tread. The dragon is sometimes described as foolhardy. Yet it is the dragon's creativity which brings good luck and great good fortune! The right brain is thus said to be the active yang side of the brain. Right-brain thinkers focus on forms and shapes, hues and subtleties, overlooking measurements and dimensions.

The left brain handles numbers, sequences, logic, organization and other matters requiring rational thought and reasoning, as well as deductive and analytical considerations. Left brains seemed more at home with things mathematical and scientific. Left-brain thinkers focus on lines and formulae, ignoring the subtleties of colour and cadence. *The left brain is the cold analytical tiger* who is ruled more by logic than by creativity. The tiger is never foolhardy. He is always careful. He represents the yin side of the human individual.

It was discovered that people trained more or less exclusively to use only one side of the brain often found it difficult (and sometimes even impossible) to use the other side of the brain. Thus those educated to think logically and sequentially, to the total exclusion of creativity, seemed to have limited ability to think outside their rigidly set rational boundaries. So they had become single-dimensional in their thinking! Such people are said to be excessively yin in their outlook. Their inner feng shui is out of sync.

Similarly, artists who had never been taught or encouraged to use their rational logical minds could be tremendously skilled painters or designers but they seemed hopelessly inadequate when called upon to undertake work requiring sequential or analytical input. Such people were excessively yang. This is why divas, prima donnas and other creative geniuses of the performing arts are often so hot-tempered. They generally exhibit traits that reveal an excess of yang energy.

More significantly, it was also discovered that when the less used of the two brains was somehow activated, through stimulation and encouragement, to work alongside the more often used side of the brain, the end result was often far superior in overall efficiency and effectiveness. In short, the two brains working simultaneously produced better results. This reflects the wholeness of yin and yang in perfect balance and harmony. This manifests in perfect alignment of chi, which results in superior performance.

These scientific revelations about the structure and functions of the human brain have special significance for those who need to be convinced of the exact nature of the brain's capabilities. Thus science confirms the need for balance in the activating and usage of the left and right sides of our brain. Neither should be exclusively favoured. Good fortune cannot be achieved that way. Everyone should develop both sides of the brain: both categories of thought processes, left and right, should always be energized, through usage.

> **Equal billing must thus be given to the**
> **two dimensions of human thought,**
> **creativity alongside reason,**
> **the dragon alongside the tiger.**

You can be scientific or artistic or, better still, you can be both. You just need to develop your brainpower accordingly. There is no such thing as an inherently unlucky person. Everyone has it in them to create great good fortune in their lives, to attain heights of brilliance and to carve out a prominent place in any field of endeavour. Everyone can be a success. The raw material exists in every person. It only has to be activated and energized for this potential to be realized and nurtured into glorious achievement. This is a fact. It is not an opinion, and no one need ever again believe it when someone describes them as stupid, unlucky, born to fail or a loser.

Everyone is a potential winner, a potential genius, a potential millionaire.

In the past, traditional recognition of brilliant minds centred on the academic or intellectual. Educational excellence, especially of the Western variety, focused almost exclusively on the three Rs – reading, writing and arithmetic – all requiring tiger brain thought patterns. Those who lacked these abilities, and instead showed prowess in skills which reflected their dragon brain bias – music, art, sports, handicrafts – were often dismissed as less intelligent, less likely to succeed in life. Except of course for the handful who somehow cut through prejudice and gained recognition. Parents indiscriminately discouraged development of the dragon brain by pushing their children to strive for tiger brain excellence.

Happily, this tendency is fading away in this New Age of 'both brain' awareness. Equal billing is being given to the two dimensions of human thought. As a result we are experiencing more and more the recognition of every field of human endeavour.

Applying left and right brains

The more you use *both* sides of the brain, the greater will be the benefits. The wonderful synergy that results from the simultaneous use of the dragon and tiger brains is obvious when we see how scientific geniuses like Einstein and Stephen Hawking and great artists like Leonardo da Vinci produced their greatest theories and works of art. Einstein discovered his brilliant equation of relativity, $E = mc^2$, by combining inputs from both his brains. Likewise, Stephen Hawking combined intuition with physics to aid his investigation into the origins of the universe, while da Vinci's greatest works combined mathematical precision with artistic brilliance.

Albert Einstein – a genius who used both his dragon and tiger brains

Probably the scientific world's most celebrated genius, Albert Einstein was a renowned physicist and mathematician. He formulated the theory of relativity and changed the way scientists thought of the world and the universe! Contrary to what one might be led to believe, Albert Einstein was not *just* a tiger brain person – logical, scientific, analytical. And he did *not* formulate his brilliant theory while sitting at his desk working through his equations.

Einstein formulated the theory while taking a break from work, lying on the grass, daydreaming. As he felt the warmth of the sun, he half closed his eyes and rested. And he noticed the light from the sun filtering through half-closed eyelashes … then breaking into a thousand tiny sunbeams.

He thought to himself, I wonder, what would it be like to go for a ride on one of these little light beams? And Einstein allowed his mind to drift, taking him on an imaginary journey to the edge of the universe, to a place where his knowledge of physics told him, and nearly convinced him, he could *not* be… He had allowed his dragon brain free rein to wander into the realms of the unknown, to fly over uncharted waters.

When he awakened, a puzzled Einstein reworked his equations, but now allowing insights gained during his imaginary journey to slice gently through his formal scientific training, thereby reaching new truths. By allowing the colours and rhythms of his dragon brain to seep into the disciplined reasoning of his tiger brain, Albert Einstein made a quantum leap into space. Thus was born the theory of relativity.

Propositions arrived at by purely logical means are completely

empty of reality.

Albert Einstein

Albert Einstein was never *merely* a mathematician, or a physicist. His life did not consist only of numbers, formulae and equations. Records of his early childhood show he failed at mathematics in school, and that he was something of a compulsive daydreamer right up to college days. That he grew up to have one of the greatest minds in history must surely tell us something. He encouraged his genius to surface because he had the courage and the conviction to let his mind meander through the labyrinths of his intellect, and to take with him on his journey into the unknown reaches of the universe, his equally great and vivid imagination. Here is a man who obviously practised inner feng shui!

Stephen Hawking – another dragon and tiger brain genius

The world knows this amazing Cambridge professor through *A Brief History of Time*, in which he explains his ideas about the origins of the universe. His subject is abstract and quite beyond the comprehension of the average mind – yet this man has dazzled the world with his explanations of theoretical and quantum physics. Stephen Hawking's book has sold many thousands of copies and made him an international star. It is obvious that he practises inner feng shui for he created his own luck despite suffering from motor neurone disease.

How does he do it? How does this man of science capture the imagination of millions of non-scientifically minded people? How does a man who cannot speak and who communicates with his students and lecture audiences through a voice synthesizer, and who even looks terribly disabled, succeed in impressing both the great academic community and the average man in the street?

Listen to him as he speaks about the success of his first book:

> ... most people cannot follow mathematical equations
> – I don't care much for equations myself. This is partly
> because it is difficult for me to write them down,
> mainly because I don't have an intuitive feeling for
> equations. Instead I think in pictorial terms, and my

aim in the book was to describe these mental images
in words ... in this way I hoped that most people
would be able to share in the excitement and feeling
of achievement in the remarkable progress that has
been made in physics in the last twenty-five years.

Here then is yet another brilliant scientific mind who visualizes and who
uses both sides of his brain. Perhaps that is the secret of his great intellect.
He gives us other clues:

I would prefer to say I'm determined. If I hadn't been
fairly determined, I wouldn't be here now... I rely on
intuition a great deal. I try to guess a result, but then I
have to prove it... I quite often find that what I had
thought of is not true, or that something else is the
case that I had never thought of. That is how I found
black holes aren't completely black. I was trying to
prove something else.

Stephen Hawking demonstrates his expertise with great skill and writes
with a sense of humour. His mother has described him as having a strong
sense of wonder. He has not stopped wondering. In his latest book, *Of
Black Holes And Baby Universes*, he takes his readers still further, almost
over the limit, into his scientific high ground.

Leonardo da Vinci – a great artist

To avoid running away with the impression that only scientific minds
benefit from 'other-brain activity', one need only browse through the
works of some of the greatest artists: Leonardo da Vinci, Michelangelo
and Picasso; even some of the Impressionists. Their works do not just
indicate genius in the use of colour, in beauty of line and form, but often
also demonstrate exceptional mathematical and geometric precision, in
great and intricate detail. Here are dragon brains who also use their tiger
brains to create balance in their work.

The most outstanding example of dragon and tiger brain synchronization at work and in perfect harmony is perhaps Leonardo da Vinci. He was a magnificent artist who excelled in originality. Da Vinci's works reveal exceptional skill in mathematics and architecture. Many critics have hailed *The Last Supper* as absolutely correct in dimensions and perspective. Investigation of his sketchbooks has uncovered his phenomenal ability to visualize moving images with the exactness of a camera. His sketches of birds frozen in mid-air demonstrate his accurate understanding of the mechanics of flight.

But of course his talents were both mathematical and creative. Once again we observe the dragon and tiger brain activity manifested in the mind of a genius – this time with the genius displayed in works of art that have survived for several centuries.

What are these brilliant minds telling us?

That knowledge of dragon and tiger brains is the first step towards ensuring that we consciously activate *both* sides. Yin and yang must both have their inputs for the real genius to emerge. This enhances innate talents and skills to a considerable extent. You must actively, consciously, reach inwards towards both sides of your brain, otherwise you cannot fully appreciate the marvellous synergy that results when you combine them. Wherever the dragon is to be found, there too must be the tiger.

The structure of the brain

The brain's crumpled outer layers resemble a maze of rounded pathways made up of an intricate labyrinth of nerves, blood capillaries and billions of tiny cells. These brain cells are called neurones. Neurones look like miniature octopuses. They have a nucleus and a large number of tentacles that radiate outwards in all directions. Each of the tentacles has thousands of tiny protuberances that resemble suction pads. These, too, protrude in all directions. Scientists have calculated that the average brain contains the staggering number of *ten billion brain cells.*

Scientists have further discovered that the number of these brain cells or neurones, by themselves, does not in itself indicate levels of intelligence. What indicates intelligence (and, therefore, the use of the brain) is how the protuberances connect: each is connected to at least one other, thereby forming different patterns within the brain.

The connections are formed by means of tiny electrochemical impulses. Thus, patterns can be formed either through individual protuberances connecting with each other, or by groups of protuberances connecting with individuals or with each other. The entire brain is made up of an amazing web of interlinked patterns.

Now consider the sheer number of connections that can be made by the thousands of protuberances on the ten billion or so brain cells! It is this calculation that has convinced scientists that the average person uses less than 1 per cent of the brain. It is also this which has convinced scientists that the brain is a gigantic supercomputer.

Your own supercomputer

If you attempt to calculate the number of connections between the individual protuberances of the tentacles of the ten billion cells of an average brain, you will begin to appreciate the enormous number we are dealing with. These connections are what form the *relationships* between all of the bits and pieces of information and knowledge that ultimately make up what we call human intelligence.

Every time the individual learns something, remembers something, experiences something, links are made between these protuberances. Over a lifetime, these millions of connections make up the individual's utilization of the brain. Try to picture the connections. Try to visualize how the mind functions. We are told that these vital connections occur as a result of the electrochemical impulses that occur each time the brain is used.

We can take 'using the brain' to mean 'thinking', and at a more advanced level of thinking, 'concentrating'. The more we use our brain, the better it becomes at creating additional success potential or what we can term good luck, intelligence, cleverness … use any word you like, they all lead to the same result. Similarly the more we concentrate, the more we improve the usage of the brain.

It should not be surprising that respected intellectuals, teachers, professionals and so forth – successful people – are those who have succeeded in using their brain to a high degree. The key to unlocking our success potential is so simple: just use your brain as much and as often as you can!

Or put another way, just *cause* it to be used as much as possible. For of course the brain cannot function by itself. It needs to be stimulated by electrochemical impulses, or thoughts. They need to be activated by the mind!

A simple enough thing to do if you make a mild effort. It requires no physical effort to cause the brain to be used. And yet it is surprising how few people have either the inclination or the wish to do so. Mentally lazy people dislike thinking, or make it a habit to delegate their thinking to someone else, so that over a period of time their brains get weaker, and they give up control of their minds altogether.

This is how chi stagnates in the brain. This is how the secret poison arrows that send out killing chi are created. Brains which are not energized and not used are storehouses of bad chi. People who suffer from this affliction are badly in need of inner feng shui. For them success is an elusive word and happiness seems really hard to come by. Such people lack motivation, purpose and goals in their lives, and they get into a fearsome spiral of negative feng shui. For such people, even when they live in homes that have good energy, the bad energy they themselves carry along with them will cause all the good chi of the house to become contaminated.

You must not let this happen to you. *Your brain is a precious thing* – as precious as your mind. These are the tangible and intangible tools of inner feng shui which have the power to create excellent good fortune for you. Nurture these tools. Don't ignore them. Don't let them gather dust. Use them.

It is like physical exercise: the more you do it, the healthier your physique. When you stop exercising, your muscles lose strength and flexibility. What this means is that every form, every variation and every manifestation of the luck you create for yourself is within your own control. You have to make use of your brain by making the fullest use of your mind. You can decide to keep it hidden and unused or you can nurture and develop it until it becomes the real secret of your success.

In the process you can make yourself as lucky as you wish!!

The upper and lower brain

There is another aspect of brain structure that adds to our understanding of the brain and this is the discovery of the upper and lower brains, and the nature of their relationship to each other, and to the physical body.

The upper brain is often referred to as the thinking cap! The upper brain can be described as the 'intellectual' brain. It deals with the many variations of intellectual activities related to practical everyday exertions. More important, it is the conscious brain, in the sense that it controls conscious, premeditated activities of the person. It also regulates all the voluntary body functions: for example when you give the command to stand, or to sit, it is the upper brain which sends the signals to the muscles that make you stand or sit. The dragon and tiger right and left brains are part of the upper brain.

The lower brain is the subconscious brain. It controls the emotions, the attitudes, the instincts. It also controls all of the body's involuntary and automatic functions: the pumping of the heart, the temperature, the blood pressure, the digestive process and so forth. It is the lower brain that connects with your awareness, in that your feelings, your moods, your attitudes, your perceptions and your expectations all get processed here. The lower brain connects directly with the mind, and operates independently of the upper brain; the upper has no control over the lower, and vice versa.

One cannot consciously change the rate of one's heartbeat. Or reduce the temperature of one's body. Or stop the flow of blood to different parts of the body. But the lower brain *can* be controlled by the mind if you know how. Control over the lower brain assumes that you have good control over your mind.

The upper brain was assumed to have absolutely no control over automatic body functions. In 1970 an Indian yoga master proved otherwise. Swami Rama demonstrated to the Meninger Foundation in Kansas that he could quite easily control his body with his mind. In a series of experiments, sitting still, and using just his mind, he created temperature changes within his body, stopped his heart from pumping blood and even changed the speed of his own brain waves!

Swami Rama's performance convinced the researchers that there were mind techniques that could lead to control of the lower brain.

Different perspectives from Eastern mystics

In the closing decade of the previous millennium we witnessed an explosion of conscious mental development. In the coming centuries the great leap in awareness of our inner space consciousness will focus more and more attention on the mind. Exploration of the mental cosmos has already started, by scientists and spiritualists alike. It will not be surprising if, very soon, someone somewhere discovers a way of accelerating those vital connections in the brain. Who knows then what quantum surge in new knowledge the human brain will come up with?

The yoga master's extraordinary control of his involuntary body functions opened new frontiers for brain research. If the upper (or conscious) brain can indeed control the functions of the lower (unconscious) brain, then *surely* the upper brain could in effect control the body's physical health, could cure diseases and malfunctioning of the body, could even push the body to limits of athletic and aerobic performance.

And maybe other things as well! It was this aspect of the brain's ability that first put the spotlight on Eastern spiritual and mystical practices, such as breath control, meditation and mental visualization techniques. Since then, a veritable deluge of investigative work on these practices has created what is now called New Age awareness. This has focused attention on the power lying dormant in the human space consciousness.

New Age gurus speak of vigorous, hidden, and as yet untapped forces inside us. They refer to the immense power of the subconscious mind, to the potency of mind programming, to the vigour of premeditated subconscious motivation — taking their cue from the wealth of teachings culled from various Eastern spiritual practices — the 'magic' of the Sufi mystics of Persia, astral communication from Tibet, yoga breath control from India, mind meditation from Zen and other branches of Buddhism. And most significantly the practice of feng shui on all levels of consciousness. By taking control of our earth and mankind luck (*ren chai*) we generate auspicious and prosperous chi, which arises both out of the land and out of the human mind itself. Research into the brain's vast capacity and potential has now extended to the mind, and in later chapters we turn the spotlight to the techniques for energizing the feng shui of the mind.

2.

Tuning into the mental space consciousness

Develop awareness

Tune into your mental space consciousness.

Watch your mind as it creates

The moods and patterns of your life,

Watch as it creates your perception of good and bad
   fortune.

Imagine a tree with branches coming out from the main trunk and then separating into more and more branches. If you have ever seen a tree devoid of leaves in the winter, you will get a pretty good idea of what thought processes would look like if you were to make a pictorial sketch of them. Now imagine that every branch is a thought, and every branch of the first branch is a branch of that first thought.

Everything you think about always leads to another thought. Every feeling you feel leads to another feeling. So you can carefully trace your thought along as it twists and turns. Sometimes, one thought simply jumps to another totally unrelated thought. Think of it leapfrogging to another branch. Remember that thoughts are often the end result of past programming. So thinking can be voluntary or involuntary. It can be premeditated or spontaneous. It can be happy or sad. It can be light or heavy. And it can be bright or dark. It can in actual fact be anything!

The power to control your thoughts lies within you. It is this power that will make inner feng shui bring the most auspicious developments into your life. Negative unhappy thoughts cause you to create a state of unhappiness, and the depth of your unhappiness is completely based on the intensity of your unhappy thoughts. You can also produce profound feelings of happiness from positive thoughts. Oscar-winning actors and actresses have long used this technique of thinking good or bad thoughts: they use simple thought control to create the mood required by the script, often with huge success.

You can make yourself distressed, bring tears to your eyes, simply by thinking of something sad – a tragic event, the loss of a loved one, a sad movie. In the same way you can make yourself confident by thinking about your achievements, and make yourself excited by thinking of your loved one. Your thinking will control your moods. The extent of this control will vary from person to person but thoughts determine your state of mind.

Now let's look at the state of your luck. You can make yourself *feel lucky* by thinking of all the good things that happen in your life. All the opportunities that came your way, all the big breaks you got. All the accidents you missed. All the good health you enjoy. You are lucky even to be alive, what with all the wars, diseases and accidents in the world! When you adopt this perspective on life, you realize how really lucky you are.

Or you can make yourself *feel unlucky* by thinking of every bad thing that has happened to you. The toast got burnt. You slipped on the bathroom rug. You missed your deadline. You lost that promotion. You never win at lotteries. No one appreciates you. Everything that can go wrong with your life has gone wrong. Boy, you sure are unlucky!

You can compound these feelings. You can strengthen feelings of good and bad luck by adding further thoughts to them. In thinking lucky and unlucky thoughts, you can be as creative and as logical, or as unimaginative and as illogical, as you wish. No one has control over your thoughts except you.

But the end result of the direction your thoughts take – making you high or pulling you down into the depths of despair – can have enormous repercussions on how your life progresses.

Thinking lucky thoughts bring you good luck.

Thinking unlucky thoughts brings you bad luck.

It is as simple as that!

It is only by controlling your thoughts that you can control your feelings, your moods, your emotions, and your conviction about whether you are having good or bad luck. Pause now and *tune in to your thoughts*. Look at what you are thinking of now… If your mind has wandered off, bring it back to the words you are reading.

An exercise in thinking

Now think of something that is important to you – a person, an event, a recent development – and let your thoughts flow with no control over them. Give yourself a few moments and then start to watch your thoughts.

By doing this, you can embark on an appraisal of your own thought processes. Try it. Do not exercise any voluntary control over your thoughts. Just let them flow.

Remember, each time you *think*, you are activating electrical impulses inside your brain which cause the brain cells to connect, and connect some more. And more. The more your brain cells connect, the more they link up with other brain cells – eventually allowing you to follow a particular thought, deeper and deeper into your huge network of brain cells. When you allow your thoughts to flow freely, with no conscious effort to guide them, you are actually allowing these brain cell connections to travel any way they wish. And as you follow your thoughts, the connections take you deeper and deeper into other groups of brain cells.

If you are more of a dragon brain person, the cells of your right brain have been better used, and therefore better developed. Your thought process then takes you into the more creative, more imaginative parts of your brain. If you are more of a tiger brain person, your thought process will tend to exhibit this.

By following your thought processes, and observing them as if you were an outsider, you will be able to scrutinize the way your brain works, the way your mind moves. This is the first step towards becoming a more aware person. Think once again of the tree in winter. You are now developing mind awareness.

Do this exercise several times to make you better at it. Develop awareness and then develop sensitivity. And then develop nuances to this sensitivity. After a while you will become intensely aware of the signals your brain and your body are receiving from your mind. Make yourself sad and then make yourself happy. Do this consciously.

Make yourself feel lucky. Then make yourself feel unlucky. See if you find it easier to be pessimistic or optimistic about life. See if your thought patterns are more positive or negative. Examine your feelings. Take note of how patient you are.

It is often helpful to write down your observations about your process of thinking. Take careful note of how your thoughts move, and look at the patterns of your thought processes. At this stage there is no need to judge. Just become aware. Learn to tune in to your mind, because this is the first step to tuning in to your inner space consciousness.

Becoming aware of the 'luck' in your life

One of the most gloriously enlightening books written in recent years has to be Dr Scott Peck's magnificent *The Road Less Travelled*, a book that deals with the psychology of love, traditional values and spiritual growth, which first came out in 1990. I have read this best-selling book many times, for it opened my mind to the true nature of 'luck'.

Drawing almost exclusively on his professional experience as a practising psychiatrist, Dr Peck says:

> **Fifteen years ago, when I graduated from medical school, I was certain there were no miracles. Today I am certain that miracles abound ... and the more I look for miracles, the more I find them...**

Dr Peck says that in thinking about miracles, our frame of reference has been too dramatic. We have been looking for the burning bush, the parting of the seas, the bellowing voice from heaven. Instead we should be looking at the *ordinary day-to-day events* in our lives for evidence of the miraculous, maintaining at the same time a scientific orientation.

His way of looking at life has been a revelation for me. It has opened my eyes to the 'miracles' that abound in my own life. As he so perceptively points out, these miracles need not be large or dramatic events.

This is how we should view 'luck'. Good luck does not have to come as a bag of money, a dream job or a knight in shining armour.

Luck occurs in many indirect ways. Luck can take the form of unexplained meetings with old or new friends, which subsequently lead to a small windfall. It can come as an unexpected letter in the mail opening up a new opportunity, a chance meeting with someone which leads to a profitable new venture. Luck can be the unexplained idea *which seemingly came from nowhere* yet represents a solution to a nagging problem ... small things, but an interlinked series of them which makes life a little more pleasant.

So if you look closely at your own experiences; if you tune inwards with the conscious intention of becoming aware of the good luck in your own life, you will begin to find innumerable instances of good fortune. Think of the occasions when unexplained coincidences either saved you from an accident or caused you to come up with an idea ... or when you wanted something and then met up with someone who provided you with the means to get what you wanted.

Think hard enough about the events of your life, and you will begin to recognize a series of little lucky miracles that hitherto you missed.

You will begin to *see* and to realize that all it takes is a shift in attitude, a shift in consciousness for you suddenly to see all of these instances of good fortune! When you read in the papers about mentally disturbed or very physically sick people and begin to understand how vulnerable the human mind is to traumas, or how susceptible the human body is to the millions of germs, bacteria and pollutants in the air, ask yourself: doesn't it seem miraculous that so many more people survive and stay healthy than die of these potential killers?

What many of us overlook, in the avalanche of bad news and warnings we are subjected to daily, is that there are very many more people who are healthy than sick. There are millions of people who do *not* get sick, who do *not* succumb to diseases, whose resistance to the germs and viruses and bacteria floating around our world seem to be most efficient. Indeed it seems miraculous that we do not *all* just sicken and die... Is there a force, an invisible power within the human body that is not physical, which is protecting us all – even in the most adverse situations?

This line of thinking, this attitude which reverses the conventional approach, can be applied to almost every aspect of life. With so many cars on the road, isn't it surprising we do not have many more fatal accidents? Don't most of us lived charmed lives – escaping accidents on a daily basis? Don't most of us have such good luck?

Look again at your own life. Try to recollect the number of times you have narrowly escaped an accident, a disaster, an unfortunate occurrence – and then casually dismissed it with a careless shrug of your shoulders or a nervous giggle, *Guess I was lucky* – then forgot about it.

Dr Peck calls it the miracle of the unconscious, and he draws our attention to the two parts of our mind:

> I will frequently draw a large circle. Then at the circumference I will draw a small niche. Pointing to the inside of the niche, I say, 'That represents your conscious mind. All the rest of the circle, 95 per cent or more, represents your unconscious.' If you work long enough to understand yourself, you will come to discover that this vast part of your mind of which you have little awareness contains riches beyond imagination.

Tuning into inner space consciousness

This vast part of your mind is your inner space consciousness and, as Dr Peck says, it contains riches beyond imagination. This inner space consciousness manifests itself in dreams, in idle thoughts, in so-called slips of the tongue or in behaviour, now universally referred to as 'Freudian slips', after the noted neurologist and psychoanalyst, Sigmund Freud.

His contemporary, the psychiatrist Carl Jung, goes further, and refers to the *wisdom of the unconscious*. Jung developed the hypothesis that all of us have inherited the wisdom of the experiences of all our ancestors – what he refers to as the 'collective unconscious'. Thus he says that when we come across something that 'rings a bell' or when we recognize a place for no obvious or known reason, these are manifestations, embedded in our minds, of past knowledge and wisdom which we cannot even begin to imagine.

Buddhist masters explain this inherited wisdom as recollections from many eons of past lives. By going deep into our minds it is possible to bring forth this immense knowledge from the inner consciousness. On this basis many New Age practitioners have attempted (some with notable success) to undertake what they refer to as *past life regression*. I myself tried one of these exercises about fifteen years ago with quite amazing results.

The consensus among experts seems to be that *the inner consciousness is wiser than the surface consciousness in almost everything.* More than that, the inner consciousness almost always rules the surface consciousness, so tuning into the inner consciousness is the key to controlling the conscious mind.

Thus if your inner conscious mind is angry, the anger will manifest itself in many ways at the surface conscious level no matter how hard you may try to camouflage the anger. Likewise, when you love or want someone at the inner conscious level it can make you behave in a most peculiar way at the surface conscious level. For a complex series of reasons, the person you are at the surface conscious level may not always be the person you really are at the inner level. When you have thoroughly grasped and accepted this fact you will understand why some people are always optimistic, happy and positive, no matter what sad event may have occurred in their lives, while others always seem unhappy. The convictions and programming held at the inner conscious level are creating the happy or unhappy façade at the surface level.

It is the inner conscious mind that rules our attitudes and our moods. It is our inner conscious mind that gives us the *survival instinct* to avert accidents and avoid putting ourselves in danger. It is our inner conscious mind that protects us against illnesses and ill health. It is our inner conscious mind that creates all the good luck and good fortune in our lives.

We should stand in awe before the phenomenon of the inner conscious mind, probably one of the miracles of Creation.

To date we must acknowledge that we still do not understand how the mind works. While we can explain parts of the brain, we cannot truly understand the seemingly miraculous technology that makes the mind work. We have no real explanation for so-called psychic phenomena, for mental transmission of images and messages, and other strange manifestations of mental magic – all of which are clearly related in some way to the power of the mind's inner consciousness. Nevertheless, admitting these limits to our understanding should not prevent us from attempting to reach within.

If inner space consciousness wields such power and authority over our lives, then it really cannot be ignored. If it indeed governs how we behave, how we react, how healthy we are, how happy we can be, how pleasurable or successful we can be (and we can go on and on here), surely, then, it must benefit us to use whatever techniques have been developed by ancient mystics to unlock the power of this inner consciousness.

This is the exciting promise of inner feng shui practice. This is feng shui as applied to the mind. The first step in its practice is to develop our awareness.

We should try to understand the mind.

Techniques for tuning into the inner consciousness

All things begin with a thought. So it is also with the journey into the inner consciousness of the mind. We need to know what the mind really is.

The mind is awareness. It is consciousness. It is a non-physical kind of energy, whose function is to *know*, and to *experience*. It has natural clarity and reflects and stores everything that it experiences, in the way a clear, still lake reflects the surrounding forests and mountains.

The mind changes from moment to moment. Like a stream flowing slowly along, the mind moves from one experience to the next, reflecting in the process the totality of our many levels of consciousness. The mind is made up of thoughts, perceptions, feelings, memories and dreams. It is not a physical thing. It is not something which has thoughts and feelings. It *is* these very experiences.

The mind can be viewed as having two perspectives of consciousness:

- the *sense consciousness* – which has to do with sight, hearing, smells, taste and touch; and

- the *mental consciousness* – which encompasses the gamut of emotions, ranging from the most subtle to the most acute of feelings, from complete stillness born of contentment to extreme anger and irritation. Mental consciousness includes our intellectual processes, our emotions, our feelings, our memory, our dreams and our fantasies. Nothing in the universe is more important than the mind. Nothing can compare with it. Nothing can take its place. Everything built by humanity is mind-made. Everything had its beginnings in the minds of people.

The mind controls the body. It controls our moods, our attitudes, our feelings. From our mind emanates our sense of well-being and confidence; from it too come our feelings of fear, despair, guilt and inadequacy. It thus plays a vital role in the life of every person.

The mind should never be taken for granted.

The mind is deep and perhaps even bottomless. There is no way of even knowing how relevant is the concept of depth when it comes to the mind. What is known is that the mind has multiple levels of consciousness, and if we are to use the principles of feng shui effectively on the mind, we will need to go beyond the surface level.

So we must tune inwards to the inner levels of consciousness, and each time we should try to go deeper and deeper. For we have seen that it is the inner deeper levels that exercise control over the surface level.

Undertaking proper feng shui for the mind is essential if our life is to grow in depth and vision. We need to clean and purify the mind regularly. We need to sort the good helpful thoughts from the bad damaging thoughts that have been indiscriminately picked up and stored through the years. These are the afflictions that give out killing chi. We have to disarm the poisons that afflict the mind and cause it to grow sick. And after getting rid of the poisons, we need to strengthen all that is strong, positive and life-enhancing. This can be done using a series of techniques that create a store of auspicious chi. The energizing of the mind is done by placing strong positive thoughts into the Pa Kua of the inner mind.

This is the practice of inner feng shui, and it is not unlike mental programming. Here we are motivated by the goal of activating the mind. We will then ensure that beneficial chi – the *sheng chi* of the eight auspicious aspirations – is firmly locked in place in the Pa Kua of the inner mind.

Inner feng shui involves two principal practices:
- identifying and clearing mental poisons;
- mentally programming the eight aspirations.

Identifying and clearing mental poisons

Clearing killing chi requires identifying mental poisons and using special techniques to get rid of them. It is often a massive job. Mind can only be cleared with mind. What the mind has put into itself, only it can remove! This will take time and requires serious study and practice.

Accepting that these poisons exist and understanding that they need to be overcome and destroyed will speed up the clearing process. Tuning into the inner levels of consciousness to identify the negative poisons will then become much easier. When the will to destroy these poisons is there, it is often not difficult to get rid of them.

These poisons are the accumulation of very powerful past negative programming. Understanding even the most subtle nuances of these poisons is very important. From the time of birth, the mind has accumulated a vast storehouse of negative thoughts, reactions and responses. The poisons have gone very deep into the psyche of the mind and will not be easy to dislodge. Clearing them requires some effort and skilful application of the techniques. It also requires determination and willpower, both of which are considerably strengthened by conviction. So you must be convinced of what you are doing. The next chapter is devoted exclusively to clearing your mind of its poisons.

Mental programming of the eight aspirations

This second dimension of inner feng shui practice introduces all the positive aspirations and motivations that drive the mind towards creating wonderful good fortune. Auspicious outcomes for everything you do and in all the eight major aspirations of your life require skilful programming.

To achieve this the mind first requires exercise. It needs to be trained, otherwise it is like a wandering, fluctuating mass which flits from one subject to the next, with neither direction nor focus.

Test it out on yourself. Pause here a moment and tune into your thoughts. Become aware of the bits and pieces of things that run in and out of your mind even as you are reading this. Or, consider: have you ever read through a paragraph and suddenly realized, you have not taken anything in? An untrained mind cannot stay still. Because mind energy is so light, it flits from topic to topic. It is only when conscious and sustained efforts are made to subdue it, keep it still, that the mind begins to slow down and come under disciplined and alert control.

Making the mind stop flitting in all directions requires it to concentrate and stay focused. This is what gives it strength and power. To achieve this *focused concentration* requires a profound appreciation of the mind's strata of consciousness, so that we learn to access its deepest levels, thereby reaching its control centres.

You should also appreciate that the mind requires rest. Unfortunately it rarely, if ever, gets a chance to rest! While the physical body gets a break each time we sleep, the mind never, ever goes to sleep. Through the days and through the nights it continues to work. The only time it stops is when we stop thinking – when we have a blank screen in our heads! This is something that is nearly impossible. Because when the mind does stop working, we are either dead or we have achieved mental bliss, the state of enlightenment when everything becomes totally empty.

The nearest thing to a rest for the mind is when we succeed in attaining some measure of *relaxation*, during which time the mind slows down considerably, and gains new strength. It is for this reason that the need to develop the ability to relax is central to all the methods and techniques that have been formulated to access the mind's deepest levels of consciousness.

Levels of consciousness

The human mind is like an iceberg, made up of the surface consciousness, and the inner, submerged consciousness. The surface consciousness is the waking state that is generally referred to as the *beta level*. At this level, the degree of awareness is acute. We are all operating at the beta level when we interact with each other. We are fully conscious and awake. Our brain waves at this level of consciousness are moving at a rate of 14 to 21 cycles per second.

Like the iceberg, however, what is seen is only the tip. The inner unseen levels of consciousness are larger and far more powerful. There are three other levels – the *alpha*, the *theta* and the *delta* levels of consciousness.

The next level down from beta is the *alpha* level. This is the subconscious level where brain waves move at 7 to 14 cycles per second. It is also the dream state, the creative state and the first level of suggestibility. The alpha level of consciousness is when one is neither awake nor asleep. It is possible, in fact fairly easy, consciously to access the alpha-level inner consciousness, and at this level quite a lot of useful feng shui work can be undertaken to tap into the inner awareness of the mind's consciousness. Indeed, merely by reaching the alpha level, merely by slowing down the brain waves to this level, we have the ability to direct energy or chi flows in order to manifest desired results on the physical and surface beta levels. Yes, it is that powerful.

One level down from alpha is the *theta* level of consciousness. This is a deeper level, where brain waves move at 4 to 7 cycles per second, and this is a very powerful level for suggestibility. Much of hypnotherapy work is undertaken at this level of consciousness.

Then comes the *delta* level of consciousness. This is the level of deep sleep where brain waves are moving at 1.5 to 4 cycles per second. It is the level of total recall and total suggestibility, and it is also the level of total non-resistance. It is at this level that effective brainwashing can be successfully done.

As we go deeper and deeper into the inner recesses of the mind, note that brain waves slow down. And in the deepest levels of consciousness will be found the most firmly embedded attitudes, perceptions and fears, which rule and control our waking actions and reactions. The key to understanding human attitudes and people's different propensities continuously to attract good or bad outcomes to everything they do lies in these deep levels of consciousness. Therefore inner feng shui techniques attempt to unlock what has sunk deep into the inner consciousness.

To tap into the great store and powerful flow of chi that lie within the human mind, it is necessary to reach deep inside, to access the inner human consciousness. By controlling perceptions and attitudes at these deep levels, we gain control of the upper, waking, surface levels.

Plus, there are natural powers that seem to exist inside the human mind, powers which seem to work through the medium of *thought*, and through the medium of *pictures or symbols*. These also activate very special types of chi that touch off special metaphysical phenomena. These activated energies sometimes bring 'higher level' abilities that defy explanation and challenge conventional beliefs. This does not happen to everybody but should it happen to you, and you find yourself becoming clairvoyant or psychic, don't be alarmed. Just quietly accept your new skills and dedicate them to the good of the universe.

The inner conscious mind

The inner conscious mind controls physical human behaviour and interactions; it affects our emotions, dictates our attitudes and responses; and stores our thoughts and emotional programmes. The inner consciousness operates automatically when given the correct stimuli.

It has the power to manifest in reality all that we convince it we want. Whatever we make it believe we are, we will be. Whatever kind of luck, riches, lifestyle, ability, skill or talent we wish to have, the inner conscious mind can set the energy patterns into motion that will bring the required luck, success and skill within our reach. The inner conscious mind has the power to activate any aspiration – for wealth and success, or for health and healing – any flow of chi and pattern of energy. It is also possible to use this power to bring us the strength to cope with stress and disappointment, fatigue and despair.

The key to tapping into this power lies in the messages we send it, and the strength of these messages. We must understand this language. We must use the correct techniques and we must use them skilfully. Inner feng shui for the mind is learning the techniques of accessing the inner consciousness and then learning how to place thoughts strategically within the mind.

Internal mind chatter

Most people do not consciously attempt to communicate with their inner conscious mind. Indeed most people do not bother about the mind at all. Left to itself the mind chatters on. Thus most of us carry on an inner conversation with ourselves – about anything and everything. We observe, respond to and make judgements about problems and opportunities, the people and events around us, the things happening in our lives. Much of this internal mind chatter is directionless and unfocused. Unfortunately, a great deal of this inner dialogue is *negative.*

Because of past programming, our minds tend to exaggerate fears, highlighting our sense of inadequacy and insecurity, of inferiority and guilt. Because the messages that emanate from our inner conscious minds are more often negative than positive, it is easy to feel insecure, unloved and unappreciated. Indeed, the way we perceive ourselves is most of the time governed by a very slanted view of ourselves which includes half-truths, defensive attitudes and insecure feelings. Usually, unless a concerted effort is made to contradict these feelings, we will feel limited and constrained.

Much of our inner consciousness works without us realizing what is happening. We seldom pause to think when we automatically assume, or say, 'we can't', or 'we're unlucky' or 'we're unworthy'. We tend to overlook the meaning or long-term impact of what we are thinking or saying, seldom realizing that in effect we are programming ourselves for failure, misfortune and disappointment.

Because of this, when we feel depressed and bitter, angry, fearful or hurt – when we suffer from feelings of inferiority, humiliation, self-contempt or guilt – we find it hard to acknowledge that it is really the thoughts and convictions of our inner mind that are causing these feelings of negative self-worth. Fortunately, however, by practising inner feng shui we can *change* the way we feel – simply by changing the way we *think*. We can transform our inner messages by recognizing that we can actually place in our minds different convictions and different thoughts, thereby transforming our self-image into that of a winner instead of a loser.

3.

Mental space clearing

Every person in this world is afflicted with secret poison arrows that insidiously torture the mind and are the root cause of a great deal of worry, negative conjecture and unfortunate outcomes. These poison arrows are the source of all the problems and sufferings that cause hurt on the surface level. This is because they manifest themselves in such harmful ways.

Poison arrows in the environment cause grave misfortune and bad luck, but poison arrows that attack the mind are a thousand times worse. They are the source of all things that go wrong in your life. If you want to transform your luck and life for the better, you must seek out these poison arrows of your mind and destroy them, and the way to do this is by using the techniques of inner feng shui.

When your practice of inner feng shui succeeds in completely clearing your mind of its poisons you will have rid yourself for ever of bad luck! Poison arrows of the inner consciousness are very different from those that cause problems in the outside physical environment. Inner feng shui operates in a different realm and dimension, so poison arrows of inner consciousness are best described as abstract projections of destructive negative feelings.

It is possible broadly to categorize these poisons using three types of negative – **Anger**, **Attachment** and **Ignorance**. If you think about it very seriously you will realize that collectively, or each on its own, these three poisons represent the fundamental source of all suffering, worry and unhappiness, and all your ill fortune.

Below the surface of anger, attachment and ignorance lie a thousand ways to describe all the arrows that cause distress, anguish and bad luck in your life. It is vital that these mental poisons be dug out and destroyed. You must put all the antidotes into place in order to overcome, dissolve, block and deflect them. These poisons are like viruses which crash your life again and again!

Anger
This spoils every relationship in your life, and creates unhappiness in your

interaction with those whom you love, respect and care for. Even with those you may not care for very much, anger leads to impatience and intolerance, two negative responses that usually lead to failure. Anger leads to temper tantrums and bad judgements – which can easily result in loss of money, relationships, friendships or goodwill. Anger causes more bad luck and negative outcomes than almost anything else in the world. Anger is a most dangerous poison.

Anger is the root cause of explosive rage, which in turn causes every kind of misery and tragic outcome. Anger is manifest in abuse, violence and even murder. At its worst, anger can bring you near to the absolute collapse of your world. All the good luck in the world cannot save you from the perilous outcome of anger when it is unleashed in a particularly harmful way. If you want to enjoy good feng shui in the inner most powerful realms of your consciousness, you really should shoot down every arrow of anger in your life!

The best antidote to anger is the practice of patience. Patience is the ability to control your emotions each time you feel your ire rising. There are many ways to use patience, but they all start from the premise that you recognize that getting angry is poisonous and harmful and that anger must be eradicated. When the will to get rid of anger rises in your mind, half the battle is won.

There are three steps in the practice of patience.

- Awareness – developing alertness to angry thoughts getting out of hand;
- Reflective breathing – delaying your reaction to anger arising;
- Practising patience – changing attitudes.

Developing alertness to anger requires a constant sensitivity to your thought processes. It is not difficult to create this kind of awareness since anger almost always occurs in your interaction with other people. If you consciously make an effort to think calming thoughts before you interact with anyone it will put you in a frame of mind where you are less likely to get angry. To make it even easier, resort to the well-tried practice of making lists.

- First make a list of everything that upsets you. Many people get angry when things go wrong or not according to their plans or expectations.

- Secondly make a list of the people who are the most likely to make you angry: people you dislike, people you look down on and people you hate.

- Thirdly make a list of the times of the day and week when your tolerance level is at its lowest. Some people tend to be less tolerant in the mornings, or during the early part of the week, or late at night.

When you have created a 'profile' of your angry persona it will be a lot easier to be alert to your tolerance level of events, people and timing. The next thing to do is to analyse your angry persona. Think through the things and people who make you angry. Often just the process of thinking about these matters will go a long way towards assuaging the intensity of your feelings. This is because the mind is naturally on your side and when given a chance will, of its own accord, calm you down. When you focus *thought energy* on matters that tend to create negative outcomes for you, the mind almost automatically helps you to lessen the negative energy aligned to it. So thinking in this way eliminates the superficial cause of anger. You can then move on to the next stage.

Delaying your reaction to anger arising requires the use of reflective breathing. Practise taking deep long breaths while contemplating the anger. You can do this type of breathing while sitting or standing. It takes only a few moments. Remember to keep your spine straight.

Bring your attention to your in-breath. Follow its slow passage into your body through your nose, follow it as it moves slowly into you, going deeper and deeper until it reaches your stomach where it rests for a while before making a slow exit up your body and out of your nose. Keep following the breath as it moves in and out of you.

Do not force your breath, do not hold your breath. Here the aim is not to manipulate your breathing. What you are trying to do is to reflect on your breath as you follow it in and out of your body. This distracts your mind from any anger that may be welling up inside you. Focusing on the breath distracts the mind. It allows you valuable breathing space before coping with your anger. It allows you to become patient.

You will discover that the breath is magical. Merely by engaging your attention, your breath succeeds in calming you down. This is because the breath is in reality your life force, your life chi. Each time you call on this life force, it is practising inner feng shui. The life force never fails you when you call on it. So every time you need to make an important decision and you feel flustered because you are upset or angry about something or someone, just take a few seconds to tune into your breath. These moments spent contemplating your in- and out-breath will raise the auspicious chi like nothing else.

When you have developed the knack of delaying your reactions to anger the next step is to abolish anger permanently. The best way to do this is through constant practice.

Practising patience requires a change of attitude. This is easier said than done: it the most difficult antidote to anger to put in place. Perhaps the best way to do this is to be convinced that patience in your dealings with people requires a transformational shift in attitude. Especially when it comes to handling anger that is directed towards people.

What is this shift in attitude?

It works like this. Usually the conventional reaction towards people who annoy you, irritate you or make you angry is to avoid them as much as possible. Or you react with as much and even more negativity than the other party gives out. With the attitude of tit for tat, or an eye for an eye – righteous anger taken to predictable ends – no one benefits. Both sides lose out and bad will is the order of the day.

Change attitude. Look on these irritating, annoying, despicable people who cross your path as wish-granting gems, as precious people brought into your life solely for the purpose of allowing you to practise patience. Consider: if everyone around you is always nice, sweet, sugary and accommodating, you will never be able to do this, and if you have no practice you will never become patient. You will never overcome the poison of anger.

When this method was first put to me, I resisted it as absurd until I sat down one day to meditate on it. And then I started to use it, at first with very little success, but as time wore on I got better at it, until eventually I have found my attitude beginning to shift. So that I now actually look forward to meeting difficult people. The more I practise, the more easily I find myself keeping a grip on my temper each time something upsets me. As a result my luck with people has improved by leaps and bounds. I recognize this cannot be perfected overnight. It takes a lot of time and I am still working at it. But putting the antidote to anger in place is like placing a defensive Pa Kua mirror to reflect away all the bad vibes that anger attracts.

Attachment

Another great spoiler of lives, this is the emotion that makes you crave things, and when you have satisfied your craving, it makes you dissatisfied or afraid to lose what you've achieved. Nothing can make you happy for long. Attachment makes you desire things, objects and people.

Attachment leads to many of the harmful manifestations of bad luck – greed, lust, depression, jealousy, envy, a feeling of being deprived, and most of all an unhappiness that gets you into a negative spiral of envy, hatred, dissatisfaction and bad actions. Attachment is a huge cause of bad luck.

Get rid of attachment and you will be able to go with the flow of chi in your life. Instead of creating tension you will be creating a feeling of calm detachment. This relaxed non-attachment to objects, ideas and people is a powerful magnet for good fortune. By releasing yourself of attachment you will have destroyed the worry, pessimism and dissatisfaction in your life. Detachment gives you immense power because you are no longer vulnerable to the lure of temporary satisfactions. You will recognize that nothing gives you lasting satisfaction and that it is a waste of energy and the precious chi in you if you crave and lust after things, people or outcomes.

Note that there are three dimensions of attachment – to objects, people and outcomes – all of which require you to understand the impermanence of satisfaction. None of the three attachments will ever give you permanent happiness, and all can become the source of dissatisfaction and suffering the moment you give them too much power.

When you place the thought of detachment inside your mind, and contemplate it seriously, you will have started the process of destroying the poison of attachment. By not placing excessive emphasis on wanting something badly you immediately free your psyche of excessive yang energy. This releases blocks inside your flows of chi. It will bring what you want nearer to you.

Freeing your mind of excessive craving removes the negative energy that usually attaches to it. The surest way of attracting any kind of success is to be so confident of it coming that there is not even the slightest hint of doubt or worry that it will not come. This way not even the tiniest morsel of negative energy is attached to the thought of what you want. Detached confidence leads to an absence of mind-induced desperation and worry. There is no fear of a negative outcome because the mind knows that when you cannot get the object, the person or the outcome you wish for, it will not hurt you because there are other objects, other people and other outcomes waiting around the corner. And these alternative objects, people and outcomes may even be more pleasurable.

Ignorance

Ignorance, the third mental poison, is a major cause of despair and unhappiness that arises from a poor self-image. It is ignorance that prevents you from understanding your continued dissatisfaction with life. This is the poison arrow that makes you belittle yourself and others, makes you scoff at every good thing that comes your way; that makes you self-destructive. Ignorance blinds you to the good things in your life. It causes you to become negative about everyone and everything. It causes you to think of yourself as a born loser.

It is absolutely necessary to get rid of this poison before you can start to develop real wisdom. Only by destroying this poison of the mind can you open the door to unbelievable heights of spiritual awareness.

Ignorance is the most pervasive of all poison arrows because it is continuously being given verbal expression. Of the three poisons, ignorance is the most common cause of intense bad luck and negative outcomes. This is due to the power of the spoken word.

Words and sentences, when verbalized in a casual manner, program the inner conscious mind on a continuous basis. The mind has no sense of humour and takes everything heard or spoken in a totally *literal* sense. Thus words that relate to anyone's sense of self-worth and well-being, and which get communicated to the inner conscious mind, should always be positive. Only then can they work positively. Unfortunately this is often not the case.

The negatives

Let me review some of the very popular destructive words and messages that inadvertently get sent into the inner conscious mind: these are things we say without thinking, when we are upset, annoyed or frustrated, not realizing that the ever watchful, never sleeping mind is picking up every word:

- I can't take it any more.
- I'm sick of life.
- I can't do that!
- I'm too old for this.
- I just can't win!
- I can never understand this.
- It's impossible!

- I'm so fat.
- I can never depend on anyone for anything.
- I'm just a born loser.
- No one ever listens to a thing I say.
- I'm just wasting my breath.
- I always have to do everything myself.
- Everything I do or say is wrong.
- I guess I don't have that kind of luck.

All of the above are common enough remarks. We hear them every day, and most of the time when we say them, *we don't even really mean them.* Yet the mind has picked them up, and has proceeded to store them in its huge memory bank. So that if you say them often enough, what happens is that *they eventually become reality.*

- When you say you are fat you will become fat.
- When you say you are bored you will become bored.
- When you say you are sick you will become sick.
- When you say you are always suffering from bad luck, guess what happens?

When you understand the way your mind works, and appreciate that strong energies are created with every verbalization tossed carelessly into the inner conscious places of your mind, it should surely become easy enough to transform these loose remarks from negative to positive.

If you make a conscious effort to build up a store of positive statements, and make it a habit to verbalize these statements as frequently as possible, you will begin to see a difference in your outlook and temperament almost immediately, such is the power of verbalized thoughts – i.e. words – on the inner spaces of your mind.

Here are some case examples that might sound familiar to you:

Charlotte had been working hard all month in an effort to improve her grades at school. She wanted desperately to please her mother. In the trial exams, Charlotte felt she had done much better than the last time, that she was really improving. She was quite pleased with her efforts. When the results came out a week later, she was thrilled to see that she had improved her marks: from getting Cs and Ds, she had scored Bs in every subject. When she arrived home that afternoon, she excitedly showed her mother her results, hoping she would be pleased. Instead Charlotte's mother took one look at the report card and screamed, 'You didn't get a single A ... and you said you worked so hard.'

Charlotte's mother will probably never understand how she is systematically destroying her daughter's self-confidence and self-image; sadly, this is a most common occurrence in many households. So many parents just do not understand the great power of praise and encouragement. Instead they inadvertently burst their children's bubble so often that the message gets lodged inside the child's mind. The message that says she is stupid, inadequate and incapable of doing better *or* that working hard is just a waste of time because, over time, she has been programmed to think she just is not clever enough to achieve good grades.

John desperately wanted his wife Mary to enjoy their first visit to Europe. Having recently been promoted to the job of Sales Manager, his income had increased dramatically and he was looking forward to the European tour he had planned for them both. Mary was convinced she would be miserable. She hated the cold, she said; and she knew she would not enjoy going to museums and art galleries. Her friends had told her that these were the main attractions of a visit to Paris, Vienna and Milan. She was also sure she would not be able to eat the food there, so she brought along bottles of chillies and sauces. True to her expectations, Mary did not enjoy the trip; not only did she find the weather too cold, she also missed her rice and noodles and her legs ached from all the walking she had to do. Mary never stopped grumbling throughout the entire tour.

Poor John made a mental note never to take her to Europe again. Mary has unwittingly set herself up for much disappointment later – especially when her loving husband eventually realizes that he will find it difficult to share his success with her…

I simply don't have the energy to do anything these days! This statement was made in exasperation by Richard, an engineer, who felt that he was in a dead-end job and desperately wanted a change. Each time he saw a vacancy for an engineer advertised which sounded like just the kind of job he wanted, his immediate impulse was to sit down and write an application letter. But Richard was totally ignorant about the poisons of the mind. Each time he would crumple his carefully written application letter, because each time, his inner poisons succeeded in convincing him that he did not stand a chance, that he did not have the luck to get a better job…

Poor Richard! Constantly reinforcing his own poor self-image, he makes it worse by repeatedly planting negative opinions of himself in the inner spaces of his mind. And so afraid of having to cope with disappointment that rather than be rejected, he gives up even trying. Here, the ignorance of the mind is compounded by a self-image so negative that he spins downward in a spiral of bad luck.

When you sit down and seriously examine all the casual statements you make to yourself each day – things you say to yourself without really thinking – you will discover that much of what you say can be very negative without you realizing it. Make a note of all this negative programming you are subjecting your inner mind to. Do the same for the things you say to your loved ones, especially your children. Every time you belittle them, each time you compare them to other children, or withhold approval and praise, you are whittling away at their self-confidence.

Be honest with yourself. You will not have to think very

hard to find examples of your own negative programming.

And when you do, make a real effort to counter these negative

words and messages.

Do not be your own worst enemy! And when others say negative things to you, mentally reject it all. Say very strongly to yourself, *No I am not what he/she says I am*. Simply tell your mind to reject anything negative said to you or about you. If you make this a habit, you will find your mind actually co-operating. You will now be ready for the positives, which will act as wonderful antidotes to the huge ignorance to which you have been subjecting your mind and, by extension, your life.

The positives

Let us review examples of positive remarks that can be slipped easily into daily inner conversation patterns: casual statements we make to ourselves as we go about our daily routines. Examine some of these statements, and see if you can work them into your daily life, or better yet, try to come up with similiar messages that send positive signals of well-being to the inner spaces of your conscious mind, messages that subtly boost your self-image. Say them without thinking too much about them. Let them slip gently and unobtrusively into your memory bank:

- Hey, I feel lucky today.
- I like my boss – he's so understanding.
- Everyone's being really nice today.
- What a great day this is.
- That was such a good lunch!
- I'm really enjoying your company today.
- I'm feeling generous today!
- Business seems to be picking up.
- Life is beginning to have such meaning these days.
- I'm feeling strong and happy.
- I'm in such a good mood.

If you make the effort to do so, you will find it easy to make simple positive statements to yourself day after day. It is a very subtle form of practising inner feng shui, and because there is no stress or tension attached to these statements as you say them, you will find that, over time, they get displayed in all the correct corners of your inner space consciousness. Your mind will be strongly energized to make you feel better and better about your life and about the world. You will not even know why you feel so good. You just do.

Why? Because at the practical level, thinking strongly positive thoughts every day generates a receptive posture towards everything that happens to you. It makes you receptive to overtures, to opportunities and to new ideas. It reduces the expectation of disappointment and failure, and it surrounds you with good vibrations and makes you a fabulous person to interact with. It prepares you and sets you up for success.

So you should convince yourself that you have what it takes to succeed. But do not be so attached to the idea of wanting success that you imbue your goals with negative worry and lack of confidence. The key is to encourage through verbalized praise and approval: you can do this for yourself, or you can do this for someone you care for very much. Your child, for instance.

Nothing beats the verbalization of bits and pieces of encouragement to create a strong self-image that is relaxed enough not to be big-headed. Self-confidence is not an inflated ego. In fact, genuinely confident people are usually very humble and do not suffer from delusions at all. They are not weighed down by the burden of ignorance and wrong views. They know that the best way to attract success is to be relaxed about it, and also to be very relaxed about themselves.

Parents who constantly reinforce their children's mental well-being will bring out the best in their children. The potential is there inside every child, just waiting to be nurtured. If you are a parent, do make it a habit to guard against placing inauspicious thoughts into your child's mind. Be generous with your positive statements. When you plant positive seeds in their minds, it is like displaying auspicious symbols in all the right places. There is no greater energizer if you want your children to do you proud.

Don't forget to plant the seeds of wisdom as well. Dispel the build-up of the three poisons in their minds – anger, attachment and ignorance. Teach them from a young age by explaining and alerting them to the danger of these mental poisons. Then teach them how to cope with these poisons by placing the antidotes of strong thought patterns in their inner conscious minds. You will strengthen them enormously when you teach them the power of positive words, and show them how they can use their minds to reduce the severity of any problem that they may encounter in their life.

The mind can be used in a thousand different ways, and the way to make it effective is be convinced of its potency. Don't believe it just because I am telling you it is so. Analyse and think through what is being said here. Only with conviction in your own powerful mind does ignorance give way to the strength of inner wisdom. Outcomes and events will then be positive. When you start, you will discover that the efforts you make to overcome your ignorance of the mind will generate their own momentum.

There may be times when you lose heart and get fed up with all this talk about mentally breaking down the poisons of the mind. You may feel that your poison has nothing to do with anger, attachment and ignorance. It does not matter. Spend some time to reflect and contemplate upon your particular poison. Acknowledge your moments of distress and despondency and then let these moments pass. If you accept your feelings you will find that the simple act of acknowledgement robs them of the power to make you unhappy. Then go back to the start of this chapter and devise your own antidote based on the techniques given there to deflect the poison. But always return to being positive. If necessary, motivate yourself by mentally examining where you are at, at each moment in time.

If you do this the poison arrows will have less and less effect on your mind until one day they will simply cease to exist. By then they should be reduced to blunt instruments that no longer have the power to cause you bad luck or ill fortune. Your mind will have become much less afflicted and you can now start on reinforcing the positives. This will energize all the good things you want and bring them into existence for you.

4.

Mental programming

To practise inner feng shui effectively and comfortably, it is necessary to master the preliminaries. This means developing familiarity with some of the more common methods of mental programming. The essence of mental programming is sustained, conscious effort to reach deep into the inner mind and to place thoughts there which make it receptive to everything that makes you happy. It also teaches the mind to avoid thoughts that lead to self-destructive behaviour.

Mental programming involves a transformation of attitudes and expectations. The *born loser* syndrome is replaced with the *natural winner* instinct. Mental programming engages various exercises that get the mind used to the happy, contented and well adjusted person. Success is assumed to be a foregone conclusion. Whatever the mind sets out to do will usually meet with success, and even when this does not happen the mind has the capacity automatically to change direction.

Disappointments are viewed as temporary obstacles placed along the pathway of life. The mind is programmed to take everything that happens with relaxed detachment, never allowing success to go to the head nor failure to weaken or disappoint. Instead the mind instantly opens other doors that lead to new things. Hindrances to success are overcome; while attainments lead to further heights of achievement. When the mind reaches this subdued state you are the master of your own fate, and you will then find that the practice of inner feng shui engages the mind at increasingly subtle levels of consciousness and takes you into the higher levels of spiritual awareness. Here, success, money and material objectives recede in importance as you discover a different kind of happiness.

Mental programming is the precursor to the powerful techniques of inner feng shui practice contained in Part II of this book. Before you move on to those techniques, you should become familiar with some preliminary mental exercises.

The mind must be trained to be instantly receptive to you. Without this receptivity, it will be hard to go deeper into your mind without being confronted with blockages. I advise you to read this chapter once through before trying out any of the mental programming exercises suggested here. It is always good to understand the big picture before starting: it gives an overview and the correct perspective on what it is we are trying to achieve.

Mental programming exercises should be a source of joy. If you do them right, you will be left wondering, 'How can it be so easy?' I assure you it is. Before starting on the exercises think through the medium of your thoughts so that you see how it can be used as the central factor in doing successful mental work.

The power of thoughts

Thoughts have even greater power than words. Thoughts carry with them messages the mind interprets as truths. So that *whatever is not yet true, the mind endeavours to make come true.* Thus it is that strongly worded, positive statements can be powerful tools of inner feng shui used for transforming desires and ambitions into reality. When you control your thoughts you will have control over your mind and when you subdue your thoughts, you will have subdued your mind. This is the final goal of inner feng shui practice – to subdue your mind so that you are in control of your own destiny and your happiness at all times.

Like words, our thoughts can be negative or positive. We can distinguish the difference but the mind cannot. The mind believes what we program it to believe. Even when it is delusion we think it is real. What we think has tremendous power over what happens to us. Thoughts are all powerful.

For this reason, it is imperative to control all random thoughts in order to make certain that they do not become habit-forming, and that they do not do harm by their negativity. Mental exercise to break this habit is akin to creating an invisible and protective energy field around your mind. This protection is pervasive and powerful. It is better than all the protective Pa Kuas and other symbols that are used to guard the physical abodes of the surface planes of existence.

Probably the most effective method of creating this energy field is the regular repetitive verbalization of strong positive thoughts: the making of statements that teach the mind to react in a way that assumes a positive outcome. Regular reinforcement always leads to powerful flows of auspicious energies that work in a positive way. In addition, it affects attitudes so that responses and reactions are always positive. This creates happy and fruitful events and relationships.

Working on the mind in this way has an almost instantaneous effect. Good luck seems to manifest itself automatically. When events and people make you happy, there is no longer the need for any more evidence that good luck has started flowing towards you. Your life becomes less stressful, and you will be pleasantly surprised by the euphoria that begins to surround you. Your confidence level begins to soar. In your work you take on a 'can do' attitude, and even disappointments are no longer a source of unhappiness because the mind has convinced you that there are other directions and other opportunities awaiting you.

Mental programming exercises

1. Working on the self-image

Let's start by working on the self-image. Send a mental message to the mind that says, *I'm an OK person. I deserve good fortune. I am comfortable being loved. I accept myself as I am, totally unconditionally.* This programming convinces you to be kind and patient with yourself. And accepting yourself unconditionally, without any nuance of dissatisfaction or negativity, makes it easy for you to accept all others you interact with.

Set aside five minutes each morning just before getting up from bed. You have just awoken from sleep, and your mind at this time of day is very receptive. It is a great time to do some mental programming. This exercise does not require you to do anything but think. You can do this in bed while still half awake. Draw up a roster of mental programming exercises to suit your own personal needs. Decide if you want to do this particular self-image programming once a week or once a month. Then pick a day in that week or month and call it your *self-image day*.

Working on your self-image means discarding all feelings of inferiority; throwing away fears of unworthiness; shrugging off insecurities; rejecting defensive behaviour; and putting an end to ego-shattering criticism – either of yourself or of others. Think strongly good and positive thoughts about yourself. So think …

> I am an OK person. I am a good-hearted person. I deserve all the good luck and good fortune which comes my way. I accept everything about myself and I feel good. Every day I am learning more and more. Every day I am becoming a better person.

Reject any concept of yourself that sets limits. Limits are artificial. They can be torn down. Limits are only the illusions of your mind. Instead, create a view of yourself where all things are possible; where fear exists only to be overcome, and where life is always full of promise.

> There are no limits to all the good things that I can achieve and have in my life. I await each new day with anticipation because every day there is something that I can do to make someone happy. I am a person who is useful to the world. I have it in me to contribute to the universe in my own way. In many ways my existence has meaning.

Always think that physically, and as a social person, you can contribute to the immediate world around you. In all your relationships, use every opportunity to give yourself a boost, making it a habit to verbalize your qualities and your strengths. If you do this every day, the results will be magical.

> So this morning, my antennae are buzzing with
> anticipation. I am filled with a sense of confidence and
> happiness. I feel so good about myself that no one can
> make me feel bad today. I am very happy to be me, and
> whatever I am, I know I can make a difference to
> someone, to just one other person.

This is because it is vital for you to understand that your life is important to someone and means something to someone. Your life is useful, as much to yourself as to someone else. This knowledge gives you a strong and confident self-image, with which you can then attain any goal you aspire to.

> Whatever I am, wherever my starting point is, I can
> achieve whatever I set out to achieve. I set my
> motivations clearly. I send a signal into the universe and I
> light up my mind to become receptive to all the good
> fortune that will come pouring into my lap.

2. Mental reprogramming

The antithesis of a positive self-image is one that has been seriously scarred. Deep-rooted blockages caused by negative programming during the growing-up years often constrict the flow of positive energies. Thus *fear, guilt, resentment, anger, frustration, envy, jealousy* and all the manifestations of the three poisons are products of a lifetime of such programming. If you find yourself at a disadvantage because you feel these negative feelings a lot of the time, you must undertake the mental spring cleaning dealt with in the previous chapter.

And then you have to begin work on mental reprogramming that will free you of the negative attitudes which hold your mind captive. In the beginning, do this morning programming at least three times a week. Do it the minute you wake up. Think.

> I do have some pretty negative baggage to discard. I feel so unlucky and unhappy about everything I do. I just cannot seem to pull myself together. No one likes me at all ... *Now think of all your negative thoughts.* I know it is all in my mind ... I know these attitudes of mine have no basis in reality. I have the power to wish them all away...

This is the hardest part: convincing your mind that you do indeed have the power to push all negative thoughts about yourself out of your mind. You have to keep thinking the antidote, and thinking the antidote, in your mind until the negative thoughts disappear.

> Every negative reaction I get from others is only my perception based on my own negative thoughts. When I think that someone does not like me, it is my own thinking that is making it up. These negative thoughts are delusions creating blockages in my mind. They are all untrue. I do not need to believe them.

Keep at it because when you reprogram your mind this way, you can succeed in dispelling hostile reactions and responses to you. The rest comes easily. This is one of the most powerful methods of making anger, jealousy, blame and all negative feelings directed towards you dissipate. Think through any incident that happened the previous day and that made you unhappy, angry or depressed. In the early morning hours, when your mind is still not fully awake, think about the incident and then use strong reprogramming to dispel all negativity from the incident. Add this symbolic gesture later in the day to reinforce the throwing away of the negatives in your life:

Take a piece of paper. Write down all the things you
don't like about yourself: everything you are afraid of,
everyone you thoroughly dislike, all the times you've felt
rejected, all the people you envy. Next, go through the
list, allowing the sad stories and the self-pity to sink
right in. Really feel the negatives. Wallow in it if you
wish. *Then let go.* Burn the paper and tell yourself that
that's it – you're letting go, you're burning all the
negatives in your life ... they are gone for ever!

3. Attitude transformations

The third major programming is to transform your attitude completely.
You must consciously think to yourself that you are not afraid of rejec-
tion. You are not afraid of failure. You do not fear risks, either imagined
or real. You do not fear *not* getting what you set your heart on. For
instance, when you have just applied for a scholarship or been interviewed
for a job you desperately want, it is vital that you spend a few mornings
consciously putting the fear of the unsuccessful outcome completely out
of your mind.

Yes I do want the job so much ... and I know I have a
really good chance. But life is filled with lots of
opportunities like this. It was my positive programming
that brought this opportunity along ... so I will attune my
mind to welcoming yet more similar opportunities
coming my way ... and yes it would be great if I got this
scholarship but it is just one opportunity that has been
sent my way. I know there will be many more.

Not being afraid does not mean fooling yourself. It means acknowledging whatever fear you have and then actively programming yourself to overcome that fear. And attitude transformation means looking at the same event from a totally new perspective. When you are no longer afraid of unfavourable outcomes you will begin to adopt a more relaxed attitude, one that is free of tension.

An attitude transformation is also required when you are habitually a pessimistic person. People who want things too much almost always place huge doses of negative energy on their expectations. They allow negative thoughts to flit in and out of their minds continuously. They think of all the reasons why they should fail, so they expect to fail. The *attitudinal shift* will change all this. It will change all the outcomes in your life from negative to positive. It also improves your belief in yourself.

Consider the following thought processes expressed as seemingly simple phrases. See if you agree with these statements. If you find yourself disagreeing with some of them, ask yourself why you cannot accept them. Suppose I told you that if you believe these statements to be universal truths, that is what they will become. Are you prepared to suspend your disbelief for the two weeks it will take to convince your mind of its truth through skilful repetition and programming? When you have succeeded in becoming convinced, you will be ready to create an attitudinal shift in your mind. From the statements below select those that reflect your aspiration and repeat them to yourself for 15 minutes every morning for at least a fortnight. Better yet make up *your own 'truth' statements.*

- I can be anything I want to be.
- I always can when I believe I can.
- I can become the most popular person in my group.
- I know that increasing my income is an achievable goal.
- I can become richer.
- I can create a meaningful career out of my job.
- I can get the promotion.
- I can obtain all the necessary grades to get into the university of my choice.
- I can attract a wonderful love into my life.

- I can and will get married.
- I can become wealthy in no time at all.

4. Making a wish list

The above are common examples of mental programming, which can be adapted to almost any situation. You can make up a statement you wish were true and then systematically place it in your mind every day. Imagine yourself being given three wishes. What would you wish for?

Write down your wishes, but express them in the present tense as if you have already been granted them. Think that your three wishes have already been fulfilled. This is not a game. It is not an exercise that has been designed to entertain you. This is a serious effort to help convince you about the power of your mind. So think carefully. Make sure what you wish for is what you *really* want.

Usually, whenever I ask people what they wish for, what would make them really happy, few can give me an honest answer. Many people have no clear idea of what will make them happy. If you say to me, 'I wish for the moon', then I know you are being facetious. I know you are not honest because inherent in that statement is a conviction that your wish will *not* come true. In any case, what would you do with the moon? But, if you say to me, 'I wish for a new BMW 5 series' then I know you are serious, and I also know that you will get it if you make a statement of positive outcome every day, engaging your mind to materialize the car. This is what happened to an upwardly mobile and ambitious stock-broker I met at a party several years ago. He tried out the method I suggested and a month later excitedly called me to say that he couldn't believe it had happened but yes, he had just been head-hunted by another firm whose offer included a BMW 5 series! Except that he kept saying, 'I don't believe it, I just don't believe it. I really cannot believe it…'

Poor man, three weeks later he called to say his car had been stolen… Since he could not believe it, I told him, his car had been taken from him. By the way, this is a true story.

Making a wish list helps you to become convinced about the potency of the mind. Start with simple, easy wishes. One of the best ways to give power to your mind programming is to wake up each morning and think to yourself:

> I am always lucky. I was born lucky. For example, each time I drive into town I never have to worry about parking. I always get a parking space.

I say this in my head all the time, and I have programmed my mind to think it automatically each time I drive into town. I have never failed to find a parking space yet. So start with modest requests. Give yourself some practice before moving on to the big requests. Never treat your mind with disrespect by asking for ridiculous things... And since your mind has no sense of humour, be very careful what you ask for. It is a good idea to be quite exact when making your wish list. If you wish for things carelessly, your wish could well come true in a way that might embarrass you.

5. Recording morning wake-up thoughts

The early morning wake-up moments are usually the most effective times for undertaking powerful mental exercises. An excellent way of engaging the receptive morning mind is to keep a journal next to your bed and to fill it up with half a page of morning wake-up thoughts. Whatever it is that comes to your mind every morning when you wake up, record it immediately and as you record these thoughts, feel free to exaggerate the positive aspects. Definitely reject whatever sounds even remotely negative. Here are some examples of morning wake-up thoughts. You can use these as a guide to get you started.

> I had such a wonderful dream last night ... I dreamt of butterflies and I am sure this means I'll be having lots of visitors today...

The above is a cleverly worded positive morning thought. Below is an example of thoughts that must be changed instantly. See for yourself.

> Today's going to be a busy day. So many meetings. I'm going to be really busy. There's the meeting with the bank, and then lunch with that difficult man. I don't know how I'm going to cope. And in the afternoon, there's that awful business of the new project ... and oh dear in the evening those dreadful cocktail parties... Just thinking of the day ahead gives me a headache... I wish today was a holiday.

When you read something like this with an aware mind, a mind that has become attuned to the great value of thinking energizing positive thoughts, you cannot help but want to change these negative morning thoughts immediately. All that's required really is an attitudinal shift. Here's another example:

> Today's just another day. Same dreary life with the same dreary routine ... except today is worse. Have to take Mother to the dentist, take Sarah for ballet. That's the story of my life – I'm just the unpaid driver in this family.

Morning thoughts that start in this self-pitying mode do nothing for the mind's well-being. Now that you are getting the knack of this exercise, you should add it into your daily routine. Energize your receptive morning mind with strong positive thoughts and then reinforce these thoughts by writing them down. The act of writing thoughts into a journal engages all parts of your mind as well as your brain. The results of this journal will be phenomenal. This is because eventually you will become so good at it, you will find yourself shaping thoughts and crafting sentences that will be both outstandingly creative as well as mentally stimulating.

There are two ways to make this exercise even more potent.

- You can keep repeating your cleverly worded thought statements over and over again each morning. Thinking these every morning as you write them down is like chanting a mantra. Soon they will sink deeply into your inner conscious mind, giving them enormous strength and potency.

- Read and reflect on your morning thoughts at night. Add positive, helpful reinforcement to them. Think about them, massage them and let them flow comfortably inside your mind. Let them take root.

6. Make a date to make yourself happy

The next step in the preliminary exercises is to start to make yourself happy. This assumes that you know what will make you happy, so there is a certain amount of mental work involved here. Once a week, set aside a few moments and think through your life. At this stage it is not necessary to go too deep into meditation. Not yet. All that's required are a few moments of spontaneous thinking … about what will make you happy now, in that instant. If it is something simple like an ice cream or a chocolate bar, or to go shopping for some new clothes or to buy yourself something nice, then go out and do these things…

When you make a date with yourself each week and set aside time to get to know yourself, you will find after several weeks that you will quite naturally come to realize that there are many facets to your personality. You realize that different things make you happy at different times.

When you start to understand this, the exercise can be said to be successful.

Many of us however do not have the time to make a date with ourselves. Especially busy career types whose every waking moment is focused on their work. I know all about compulsive workaholics. Many young people these days get sucked into the system and the syndrome: there is no time for anything but impressing their bosses and working for year-end bonuses and promotions. It is a terrible spiral of potential burnout, and before they realize it they have spent too much of their prime years indoors, in air-conditioned or heated offices. Such people discover what they have lost only when they reach middle age.

Anyone reading this and finding it hard to make a date with themselves is exactly the person who needs to do it the most. Spend time on yourself in any way that makes you feel relaxed and happy. Carefully think through what you like doing and then go out and do it. If you have no idea what will make your day happier and brighter, be a little creative and adventurous.

Break out of your normal daily routine.

You can spend this time with your family; or with a friend you had been wanting to catch up with. It can mean an afternoon at the museum, a leisurely walk in the park, or a day lunching at the latest newly opened restaurant in town. You should have time to gather your thoughts and to reflect.

After you do this happy day exercise for several weeks you will get a better feel for what happiness means. It is an easy way of clarifying some important issues inside your head. The act of doing things, of taking yourself physically to places, of engaging others in your reflective world will help you think more clearly. It will help you sort through the priorities of your life.

Most importantly this exercise engages the body mind and spirit as it makes you aware of your inner and outer persona. You become aware of the way your thoughts connect with your body and your feelings. Only then will you realize how inner feng shui can become such a worthwhile thing to do.

7. Mental medicine for a wounded mind

One of the most powerfully spontaneous methods used by the mind to protect itself is selective memory. The mind simply forgets experiences that have caused intense pain, shame or grief in the past. This is especially true of childhood traumas, which are buried so deep into the hidden recesses of the mind that it takes a great effort to release them. Practising psychologists refer to these as repressed memories. So the mind develops methods to protect itself, and it uses a selective sifting process when it comes to remembering things and events that cause unhappiness.

To practise inner feng shui effectively, however, unhappy experiences must be acknowledged and confronted. Traumas of the past must be given safe and compassionate release. Minds that have been wounded and injured during the growing-up years of childhood cannot be cured if these wounds fester untreated. This way they only create hidden poisons that will eventually kill. But when they receive medicine, loving kindness and proper treatment, they get healed.

The best way of doing this is to search the mind for bad experiences if you have a phobia, a fear that seems unreasonable or hard to understand. This exercise requires you to think through your life.

Break your past into chunks of five-year intervals, and then write down incidents and experiences that stick out in each of those periods. Do not worry about structure, syntax, style or grammar. You can start anywhere, and remember anything you wish. Include good and bad experiences, and spend as much time as you wish in any period of your life. If your memories are all happy ones you are a most fortunate individual indeed. For the majority of people, the past is filled with unforgotten slights, unfairness, anger, jealousy, a feeling of being the victim, and in very bad cases, of traumatic incidents that are kept forgotten. Whatever the past was for you, if you still feel wounded by certain events then you must do something. You must acknowledge these wounds, bring them out into the light of day, wash them with your tears if need be, and then rewrite your memory of them.

If any event caused you fear as a child, analyse it in the context of what you know as an adult and reaffirm that there is no need to be afraid. If your past trauma caused you shame, anger, a feeling of uncleanness – poisonous negatives that are so harmful – expose it to the light of the present day. Rewrite the past, taking away the negatives. If some event has made it difficult for you to trust anyone today, spend time working through the hurts of yesterday. Unblock these barriers to happiness by bringing your hidden fear of trusting into the light.

This exercise is not always easy to do. A wounded mind has a fragile ego that is sensitive and easily hurt. Acceptance here is the key word. You have to convince your mind through mental reinforcement that whatever it is that caused you to hide the pain can be reduced to rubble in the light of day. Try to transform your memory of these experiences by looking for all the lessons you learnt. Think these daily thoughts to yourself:

I have learnt and I have grown strong from my past. Everything I have experienced, good and bad, has only prepared me for today, so I am able to cope with everything that comes my way now. I am strong now, stronger than I could ever have been if I had not suffered through the pain. So now I am healed. I am completely healed. My mind is healed. My personality is healed. My time for happiness has come...

8. Set yourself up for great good fortune

Practising feng shui, inner or outer, works best when you mentally set yourself up to receive great good fortune. The mind has to be receptive to success if you want to become successful. It has to be receptive to wealth if you want to become rich. It has to be accepting of happiness if you want to be happy. And it has to be receptive to good health as a way of life if you want to be healthy.

Please do not think that we are all automatically and equally amenable to good fortune. You will be surprised at the number of people who are convinced they are either not good enough or not worthy enough of receiving all the things they want. Absurd as it sounds, some people even believe it is a sin to be rich! This has to do with attitudes and expectations and is perhaps one of the most important factors that determine whether people succeed or not; whether they are happy or not.

When you set yourself up for happiness, you do everything you can to achieve this goal. You plan. You prepare. And you work. In short, you load the dice strongly in your favour by doing all you can at the conscious levels to prepare yourself for it. But you should also orientate your mind to *expect* happiness, to *expect* the achievement of your wishes in your inner mind. The same is true of success, health and wealth. To set yourself up for these manifestations of good fortune, you must work on reinforcing three important attitudes.

1. You must *believe* in yourself 100 per cent.
2. You must be genuinely *determined* to want good fortune.
3. You must strongly *expect* to succeed.

Inner feng shui can work on the mind if we have belief, determination and positive expectations. These are the three ingredients required for the mind to accept success, accept happiness, accept wealth and accept health.

Positive expectations almost always lead to positive outcomes! The human mind works in ways that can astound us, and the more we understand the mind, the more control we have over its awesome powers. When you expect to succeed, the mind establishes motivations inside you that make you work towards that success, sometimes even calling forth abilities and skills you never suspected you had. The inner mind draws on reserves of hidden energy and creativity, and propels you into action. The mind works unobtrusively and without you consciously realizing it. That is why you often ask yourself why you do the things you do, why you listen to your instincts...

It is like survival. When pushed to the limits of endurance, the surface mind is so exhausted that the inner mind takes over; it draws on special energies that give the body renewed strength to go the extra mile, take the extra step. How often have we read miraculous tales of survival! The human body can come out of many situations intact – as long as the mind stays alive and the will to live is still paramount.

It is also like a mother's protective instincts. When confronted with danger which threatens her child, a mother finds strength from deep inside her. Driven by the powerful emotion of a mother's love, the mind responds to the inner instinctive scream for more energy and releases whatever extra strength is needed to save the child.

9. Discovering the power of affirmations

Mental affirmations or statements of self-approval probably represent the easiest way of programming the mind. For those new to the power of the mind this is a no-risk way of satisfying and convincing yourself.

Using affirmations simply mean using words, thoughts, messages and statements that strongly suggest positive things about yourself. These affirmations work like personalized mantras and they enter into the belief systems of the inner mind through constant repetition and reminders. Here are some useful guidelines on working with affirmations:

- Be very clear and specific when writing out your affirmations.
- Be direct and precise in your wording.
- Keep your messages as simple and as focused as possible.
- Let your statements contain only positive messages.
- Choose sentiments and descriptions that you can honestly believe in.
- Let your affirmation contain a desire for something that you really want.
- Make sure you understand what it is you are saying very thoroughly.
- Differentiate between different types of affirmation.
- Learn the value of regular and constant repetition.
- Be very relaxed each time you affirm any of the statements.

You can be creative about the way you communicate your affirmations to your inner mind. Let them take many forms. Write them on cards, in diaries, on the walls of your room. Remember that the use of affirmations is to stimulate your mind to think in a certain way about yourself. Affirmations are the tools you can use to dissolve blockages that impede the flow of the inner chi. Mental blockages are usually far more harmful than physical barriers that stop the flow of good chi from coming into your home. You must rub out these blockages, deflect them or dissolve them so that chi flows smoothly through your inner systems. This will ensure that when you place chi energizers to activate different kinds of good fortune in your world, these have a chance to flow and to become manifest.

Affirmations counter whatever negative blocks you have. At first these positive statements give you hope, because they make you feel that maybe you do not need to believe the negative things about yourself and then they give you safety when the negative belief gets completely obliterated.

You must be prepared to meet with a certain amount of resistance from within you. Many years of deeply embedded negative attachments in your mind cannot be shaken off so easily. In the early days of verbalizing affirmations to yourself you will feel an array of feelings – from initial discomfort and embarrassment at the syrupy, saccharine positive statements to disbelief, objections and even outright indignation. But do keep at your affirmation exercises. It is a good idea to jot down the negative feelings since these often help you to work through deep-seated fears that make you resist the positive statements that you are verbalizing about yourself.

I used to believe I was ugly, and I was also extremely distrusting of anyone who praised my looks. Up until I was in my thirties anyone who started complimenting me about my appearance would make me feel extremely uncomfortable. So when I discovered affirmations many years ago, the first thing I did was wish I was beautiful. Yet each time I said those magic words 'I feel beautiful', discomfort and anger would rise up inside me. I was at a loss to understand my attitude to this simple statement.

So, through a series of meditations I went deep into my past, to the days when I was quite little, and I remember my grandmother telling me derisively how ugly I was, how dark I was from playing in the sun. I still remember her thin lips sneering at me. I must have been about six or seven then...I grew up disliking my grandmother and never understood why. When she died I was still very young, perhaps twelve or thirteen. I felt no grief or remorse. It was not until I made a determined effort to go backwards in time that I remembered all the times when she belittled me. Later when I told my mother about it, my mother revealed that she never got on with my grandmother. Maybe that was the cause of those little dramas, although it does seem unimportant now.

Once I discovered the source of my insecurity, I understood why I could never trust anyone who told me I was pretty. It was because I did not believe them. My grandmother had planted a seed inside my mind which had taken strong root until I dug out the tree of insecurity that had grown big and tall inside me. I don't feel insecure about my looks any more.

The great bonus of that magical discovery is that it released me from being overly concerned about my physical appearance. I have since then become completely relaxed with the way I am.

The power of affirmations

Affirmations are strong declarations of self-approval and favourable outcomes. They serve to confirm within us that the statement we make is already true or will become true very shortly. It is therefore one of the best ways of convincing our minds that what we respect, admire and desire most can truly become ours.

The practice of repeating affirmations is a conscious effort to replace stale destructive mind chatter with positive, encouraging ideas and attitudes. It is a powerful way of transforming our view of ourselves, our view of the world and our view of the people around us.

Affirmations can be done silently, spoken aloud, written down, sung or chanted. A few minutes of positive affirmations each morning can transform a grouchy person into a cheerful human being, a nasty bad-tempered guy into a charming hero, a weak little coward into a courageous dynamo, and a plain Jane into a stunning beauty.

Any positive statement can be an affirmation. It can be specific or general. It can cover any aspect of your life. It taps into the power of your inner mind and is one of the best ways of becoming receptive to inner feng shui practice.

Here is a series of affirmations which you might like to consider weaving into your daily morning work on mental programming. Select those you like and write them out. Then keep them next to you when you sleep so you see them in the morning. Repeat them as many times as you wish.

Self-image affirmations

I FEEL GOOD ABOUT MYSELF

This is an affirmation that helps you tune inwards into yourself. The goal is to create a positive self-image that effectively counters feelings of inade-quacy, inferiority and insecurity. When you send positive signals to your inner mind, the implication is that you accept yourself – totally and uncon-ditionally. You accept the way you look, the way you are made – your social status, your race, your colour, your sex, your weight. Accept every-thing about yourself and your circumstances which you cannot easily or immediately do anything about. This clears the way for whatever you may wish to do to improve yourself.

I BELIEVE IN MYSELF

Ultimately, all your affirmation programming can be successful only if
you have faith in yourself. If your affirmations are half-hearted or shaky,
the inner mind is not convinced. So be strong. Tell yourself as many times
as you like that you believe strongly and totally in yourself. Say it when
doubts start to surface; or when you feel alone, afraid and despondent.
Trust yourself completely because this is the only way to reach that
something deep inside your nature. Trusting yourself unlocks your innermost precious store of chi, and by reinforcing this sentiment daily, you
will be giving it strength and power! Believing in yourself is one of the
best ways to inspire yourself.

I CHOOSE TO BE FREE

Being free means discarding the need for self-flagellation and self-criticism.
No need for role playing and putting on a false front, especially to yourself,
but also to others. No need to constantly have your self-worth defined in
terms of other people's expectations and other people's approval. Bestow
upon yourself the gift of self-esteem. Do not let your happiness and sense
of well-being depend on having to please others. And don't let it depend
on others pleasing you. Let your personal happiness be a function only of
your own feelings of worth. Choose to be free. Actively shake off the
shackles of mental restrictions. If you keep programming yourself this way,
you will find it increasingly easy not to judge or criticize others. And when
others criticize or judge you, you will find it equally easy to accept this with
all the grace in the world. Your feelings of self-worth will stay intact.

Confidence-building affirmations

I CAN. I CAN DO ANYTHING

I can do anything is probably the greatest confidence-building statement in the world. So much talent and achievement are lost to the world simply because so many of us doubt our own abilities. The fear of failure, of losing face, of losing money, of the unknown, are such effective deterrents that those caught in its spiral fear even to try or make the effort.

'I can do anything' or simply 'I can' is such a simple little message, yet so powerful. To those who would argue that it is foolish to ignore one's limitations and who therefore do not accept the 'I can do anything' credo, just be reminded that this affirmation is meant to increase your determination and self-confidence. Sure, not everyone has it in them to become Prime Minister; it is mentally healthy to acknowledge one's short-comings and limits. Nevertheless, I ask you – if you don't try, how will you know what you can or cannot do?

When you say to yourself, regularly and with conviction, 'I can', you are in effect mobilizing yourself to make the best of your own resources, and doing everything in your power to realize your full potential. The statement 'I can' will galvanize you into action by building your confidence and strongly increasing your determination and persistence – key ingredients in the pursuit of success!

'I can' also increases your energy level. It makes you focused and concentrated because in saying it you automatically think of the goal you have in mind.

When you say *I can do anything!* the mind asks, 'Do what?' The inner mind will have the answer if you have thought through your ambitions. The statement activates all of your inner resources, targeting them towards satisfying what the mind now knows it has to do.

My country, Malaysia, is a small country that lies at the south-eastern tip of the great continent of Asia. The motto of my country is 'Malaysia boleh' which means 'Malaysia can'. This slogan is repeated on television, on radio and in the press every day and it has done wonders for the country. I feel a real sense of pride when I read the great feats of endurance to which this slogan has inspired my countrymen. No, I am not talking about economic wealth and progress, although we have that aplenty. I refer to that small group of mountain climbers who successfully scaled Mount Everest; to that lone sailor who braved the oceans when he single-handedly sailed round the world; to the creative designer who went to New York to make a name for himself – and many more.

Success and achievement can come in any field of human endeavour. It can come at any age, and at any time. But we can only when we believe we can!

I can focuses beautifully on the goal. For sportsmen, or for those who find themselves in need of that precious last ounce of energy, repeating this phrase in the head sends a message to the mind, which immediately activates everything in the body to prove the statement true. So if it is becoming a winner, completing a race, going for a job, standing for an election, applying for a scholarship – anything at all that occupies your mind at any moment in time, say *I can* to yourself fervently and with conviction. Let your mind actualize positive results for you!

I LIKE MYSELF

'The love of oneself is the start of a lifelong romance,' said Oscar Wilde! And indeed, unless you love yourself, how can others love you, and how can you love others? Unless you are secure in the knowledge that you are attractive enough to deserve your own devotion, how can you convince others of this?

To move with confidence, you have genuinely to appreciate all that you are. This does not mean being narcissistic. It does not mean having a king-size ego. Loving oneself to create a positive self-image is completely different from the self-cherishing mind, the mind that is self-centred. Loving yourself is accepting the way you are and not spending your life wishing for what you are not. Saying 'I like myself' does not suggest vain conceit and gullible glorification. On the contrary, it is only the insecure who need superficial trimmings and ego boosters. When you genuinely like and appreciate yourself, it breeds a solid sense of security that has no need of these things.

Self-confident people are stunningly free of silly (and destructive) chips on their shoulder that are caused by deep-seated insecurities. So make an effort to like yourself, and repeat it day after day. Each time you feel like finding fault with yourself, pull this statement into your mind and repeat it.

Always be aware of subtle put-downs. Reject them categorically the instant they surface in your mind. Counter immediately with the message that you like yourself. Over time, this continuous programming will nurture your sense of self-worth at the deepest levels of your mind. You will become more confident. You will accept yourself unconditionally.

Whatever failings you may have (and all of us have failings) should not detract from your sense of self. Whatever you may need to do to improve yourself – acknowledge and go about making the improvements. But in themselves, failings are not reasons to flagellate yourself. The love of oneself, to be powerful and pure, must be totally unconditional! Just as the love for others should be totally unconditional. This is a powerful truth deserving of some meditation. Start programming it into your mind.

I FEEL TOTALLY CONFIDENT

This is a straightforward statement that directly addresses one of the most vital ingredients of good fortune and successful interpersonal interactions. Being confident is a state of mind – the result of the mind's unconscious conditioning during the growing-up years and beyond. Confidence is one of the most important aspects of personality. Without confidence, the world, and everything in it, is a steep and unfriendly mountain where wild animals freely roam waiting to kill you.

Lack of confidence is the result of, and also the cause of, phobias that cripple the personality. What come across then are shyness, cowardice and the expectation of non-acceptance, dislike and failure. People who lack confidence are pathetic in their interactions with others. They project a loser image, a *kiasu* attitude. Confident people come across as strong and reassuring. Their auras give off a glow of energy that is infectious and vivacious. They project a warmth that reflects their inner self-assurance, something most people find attractive and even inspiring. For them, the world is a long happy rollercoaster ride, one easy mountain after another.

I AM IN FULL CONTROL

Confidence comes only when there is the conviction that we are in control of our lives and our feelings. Control here is a key word. When you are in charge you are less subject to mood swings. You are also much less temperamental because you have the ability to take charge of the way you respond and react. Your feelings do not easily run away with you: you are less likely to be ruled by your emotions. People cannot easily upset you. Events do not easily disturb you, and disappointments will not easily conquer you.

Deep inside, you know that you control your own destiny and the outcomes in your life. You know that as a living, breathing human being, you have the choice to fight or to take flight. You are in control! This is the best form of confidence – the most efficient way of tapping into your own inner resources. When you say, 'I am fully in control', you acknowledge that you are the master of your life, and of your thoughts and attitudes. It is a fantastic way of tapping your inner power!

Strengthening affirmations

I AM STRONG AND HEALTHY

When you keep telling yourself how strong you are, you will become healthier; your energy levels will get a huge boost, and physically your body responds by getting fitter and stronger. This affirmation will make you nurture and look after your body – making sure it gets enough exercise, enough nutrients and enough rest.

But strength does not only refer to physical prowess and energy levels. Mentally too your faculties will get a shot of adrenalin. You will have greater staying power and become more resilient. Strong people do not bend with the wind. They are not easily influenced. They do not depend on others for their sense of self-worth. They do not need the constant approval of others. Strong people have the courage to be themselves, to take some risks, to hold an opinion, and to follow their own judgement and instincts. Strong people are also never afraid to learn from others. Because they are strong, they can more easily accept alternative and contrary views. This is because their strength comes from the inside. When you repeat the statement 'I am strong' you are in effect programming greater courage into the inner consciousness of your mind. By building inner strength this way, you will always be prepared to face any new challenge or disappointment. Having internal strength means you have armed yourself to cope effectively with whatever life brings.

I WILL NOT BE VANQUISHED

This is a stirring message, which helps the mind cope with disappointments. It is an affirmation that inspires the inner mind to stand firm and solid in the face of adversity or tragedy. When confronted with cash problems in a business, or when one has lost a loved one, feelings of helplessness, inadequacy and even terrible sadness can sometimes immobilize even the strongest of people. If you are going through just such a time, and you need strength, try repeating this statement to yourself. Tell your inner mind that you will not be beaten, that you can and you will pick yourself up again. From somewhere deep inside you then will spring wonderful reserves of energy to carry you triumphantly through your difficult period.

Predictive affirmations

EVERY DAY I AM GETTING BETTER AND BETTER

One of the most mysterious aspects of the mind's capabilities seems to be its ability to actualize all that it expects to happen. The lifestyle and life situation that materializes depends on what the mind believes.

Predictive affirmations work really well when uttered with relaxed conviction; they can be as broad-ranging or as specific as we wish. And they can refer to events or to people or even to one's own ability. 'Every day I am getting better and better' is a powerful all-inclusive statement which strongly conditions the mind to bring about steady improvement. If you incorporate this statement into your daily internal conversations, you do not even need to spell out what improvements you are looking for. The mind will dig into your innermost desires and compel itself to realize these improvements.

Remember that the mind, aided by the brain, is a supercomputer. Everything that you secretly wish for and want has already been registered in its memory bank. The mind knows what will make you happy; what abilities you wish you had; how you desire to improve. This statement merely activates the button that will get you started along the road to getting better and better. It will motivate you to do all that needs to be done.

I EXPECT TO SUCCEED

The expectation of success sets up positive vibrations in the mind that create a transformation of attitudes. This in turn attracts success chi that spurs you on to higher levels of achievement. Expect success, it is said, and you will get success. Expect to fail and you will fail. The mind is very literal in its interpretation of what it is told. It believes what it hears, and acts accordingly. This is why it is so dangerous to be negative. By all means anticipate what can go wrong and plan for eventualities – but never expect bad things to happen, things to go wrong. Be careful and be prepared, but always expect and hope for the best possible outcomes. Your mind generates powerful energies. Let these energies be auspicious and ensure that your mind helps rather than hinders you.

Skillp-enhancement affirmations

I'M GETTING REALLY GOOD AT THIS

When striving to improve at a skill – at sports, at playing a musical instrument or drawing, or when studying for a professional qualification of any kind – it is always useful to engage the power of the mind fully. By doing this you tap into your inner resources, so that learning takes place at both the surface conscious and inner subconscious levels. Convince your mind that you are moving steadily up the learning curve and you will make quantum leaps ahead.

When you consciously support your studying and learning efforts with this kind of positive mental programming, the process becomes easier, more satisfying, and definitely more fun. If you like, you can also create a complementary predictive affirmation that lends greater credence and strength.

But as with the other affirmations, for it to be effective you must repeat it regularly and with conviction. Set yourself up for success. Do not sabotage your programming efforts by looking for reasons why you cannot improve – *no time, too old, too tired, no energy* – these negatives subvert the learning process. Believe you have hidden talent and untapped potential inside you – then allow it to surface. You will often be surprised at what you are capable of.

For students working towards getting good grades in examinations, this is one of the most effective affirmations to incorporate into their daily subject programming. Before doing homework or sitting down to revise a subject, just say this affirmation repeatedly, and with no tension, before and after the study session. It will vastly improve the mind's receptivity to the input of new knowledge. Not only that ... if the mind is programmed beforehand, the brain works more efficiently in retention and recall. The end result is that improved learning takes place.

Stress-reducing affirmations

IT IS SO EASY TO RELAX

One of the greatest causes of stress is the inability to relax.

Even when asleep, few people are able truly to reach deep levels of sleep that allow their minds to rest. As a consequence, stress, and diseases caused by stress, afflict too many people, especially those engaged in high-pressure jobs. To counter this, affirmations can be used to persuade the mind to take an occasional rest. Of course there are special techniques which can be learnt and practised – techniques of meditation and mental quieting that not only succeed in profoundly relaxing the mind, but also allow it to reach consciously into the deeper levels of consciousness. Affirmations are another powerful way of making the mind relax. Merely by telling the mind it is easy to do so ensures that each time you wish to close your eyes and take a five-minute break, you will be able to do so.

I AM COOL, CALM AND COLLECTED

This is an important affirmation for workaholics engaged in high-pressure jobs. Stress caused by tension, ridiculous deadlines, absurd expectations, constantly changing signals and all kinds of demands made at work. These can build up until those unused to this level of pressure explode. People in this sort of situation really need calming affirmations like this.

Calming reassurances addressed to the mind help it keep its cool. Those who suffer from explosive tempers would do well to program their minds with this affirmation. It may save them from the dangers of high blood pressure. This affirmation is excellent when accompanied by deep breathing. The breath is a magical tool which helps you to focus inward. So say this statement while taking slow, deep breaths.

I CAN COPE EASILY AND EFFORTLESSLY

A major cause of stress is the inability to cope with the multitude of demands and pressures that claim our attention. This kind of stress is especially bad when a huge crisis at work is compounded by other things going wrong at the same time. As Shakespeare pointed out in *Hamlet*, sorrows usually come not as 'single spies but in battalions'.

If nothing is done about it, this kind of stress can lead to ulcers, migraines, blackouts, and in extreme cases can even lead to suicide. It is almost vital for people in high-stress jobs (like dealers and traders) to keep repeating this statement constantly to themselves. It should even be given mantra status, by being repeated at least a hundred times each day.

By convincing the mind it can cope easily and without effort, what is normally stressful can be dealt with. Again this is an affirmation that works well with deep, slow breathing.

Special affirmations

MY LIFE IS BLOSSOMING IN TOTAL PERFECTION

This is a feel-good affirmation which creates marvellous vibrations about the future. It is also one of those life-enhancing statements that inspires faith in oneself. It sets the mind to expect all kinds of good things.

EVERYTHING IS COMING TO ME EASILY AND EFFORTLESSLY

This is a reassuring affirmation, which once again sets the mind to expect success in all endeavours. Focusing on how easy things will be describes a life free of stress and worry. It is a fabulous affirmation and is one of my all-time personal favourites. I have been repeating this mantra for as long as I have used mind power.

MY FUTURE LOOKS ROSY AND FULL OF PROMISE

This high-expectation affirmation effectively conditions the mind to believe it has wonderful things to look forward to, thereby encouraging it to open its doors wide for fresh opportunities to come in. All things bright and beautiful are suggested by this affirmation. This too is one of my favourites.

EVERYTHING IS WORKING OUT FOR ME PERFECTLY

This all-embracing statement brings comfort to the troubled mind even as it banishes deep-seated worries that cause negative vibes to rear their ugly heads. Whenever things do not work out as planned, and one is tempted to speculate on all sorts of outcomes, repeating this affirmation establishes the signal for something good and positive to be the end result.

I AM A RADIANT PERSON, FULL OF LOVE AND LAUGHTER

This is a self-inspiring statement which helps all the best inner qualities we secretly possess to see the light of day. It makes for a brighter, more vivacious personality, and it attracts new people into our lives.

I AM ATTRACTING LOVE, LUCK AND WEALTH INTO MY LIFE

This strong predictive statement contains plenty of optimism for the future. It is a bold and direct assault on the mind, compelling it to view life through rose-tinted glasses. Not everyone can use this statement with conviction, but for those who can, its effects are both powerful and extremely comforting.

This statement is riveting for those who believe in fortune telling, astrology and the like: it is just as easy to predict a wonderful future for yourself! You can be your own fortune teller. *You* can be the one to interpret the cards.

I am one of those people who adore having my fortune read. The difference between others and me is that I have programmed my mind to hear only the good things, to remember only the promise of wealth, success and happiness. Anything bad, I simply extinguish with instant forgetfulness. Looking back, I realize that it has only been the good things predicted which have happened. As for the difficult times, I have simply forgotten them, and even if they have occurred – and they must have, since we all enjoy cycles of good and bad luck – my mind simply views them as temporary hiccups!

Anyone can do the same. To a very large extent, we create our own reality. We have the freedom to choose. We can either colour the events in our lives with broad welcoming strokes, always seeing only the promise of better things to come, or we can be defeated by the fear of dreadful and negative outcomes. By repeating the affirmation, 'I am attracting love, luck and wealth into my life' we set the stage for a magnificent future full of promise. We set the stage for practising inner feng shui with great success. Mind programming will make you a more relaxed, happier, richer and more healthy person.

Satisfying the lower chakras

When you use the power of the mind to complement the practise of conventional feng shui you will reap a harvest of good things, which will satisfy the three lower chakras of the human body. These lower chakras, or intense energy centres, dominate the outer senses.

The root chakra links the person with the physical world. It defines the concept of being and serves as the foundation from which the self evolves its identity. The root chakra encompasses aspects such as external chi, ambitions, desire for security, love and survival. The colour of the root chakra is red and its symbol is the four-petalled lotus. The energy centre is between the genitals and the anus. Its element is earth, and satisfying this chakra centres around love, family and security. The root chakra has a calming influence. It is the basis of perceived good fortune. The practice of environmental feng shui, strengthened by mental programming, reinforces this foundation of the self and prepares the way for the practice of inner feng shui.

The lower abdomen chakra is the centre of sexual energy, creativity and raw emotions. This focuses on sexual gratification, which creates the flow of chi between lovers and spouses. The colour is orange and the symbol is the six-petalled lotus. Satisfying this chakra makes it easier to move to the upper chakras. The element of this chakra is water.

The solar plexus chakra is positioned in the centre of the body. Its impulse is desire and it is here that all the material senses are satisfied – for food, affection, security, family. All aspects of the personality are centred here. Many masters from India tell me this is where the earthly and heavenly chi mingle in a golden yellow haze. The symbol is the ten-petalled lotus and the element is fire. This is the third of the lower chakras, and as energy reaches this part of the body it gets ready to enter into the realms of the spiritual or upper chakras, the first of which is the heart chakra. This is then followed by the throat chakra, the third eye chakra and the crown chakra. These four chakras engage the spiritual senses and inner feng shui work awakens the upper chakras. Many feng shui masters have advised me that it is very difficult really to satisfy the upper chakras unless one has either fully satisfied the lower chakras, or at least has attained such high spiritual awareness that the satisfaction of the lower chakras becomes irrelevant.

I have discovered this observation – passed on to me by very learned Taoist masters as well – to be true, at least in my own life. The practice of inner feng shui is best engaged after one has achieved a certain satisfaction with one's material life. This satisfaction gives rise to a relaxed but powerfully aware mind, which is the state of mind that benefits most from the practice of inner feng shui.

Part II

5.

Simple meditations for inner feng shui practice

Meditation is a lot less difficult than most people realize. It is a quiet mental activity, which can be done sitting, walking or lying down. Meditation can be simple five-minute exercises of the mind, or it can be very prolonged sessions of mental mindfulness that can go on for days and even weeks at a time. In addition to facilitating the practice of inner feng shui, meditation has a thousand other uses and outcomes.

I am told that many holy lamas sit in meditation for months and even years without the need for sustenance. These holy men of the mountains are such highly realized and skilled yogics, they do not even require warm clothing in the sub-zero winters of the mountains – their bodies create so much natural heat through intensive meditation.

For us rank amateurs in mind exercises, it is enough that we attain the kind of meditation that takes us successfully into our inner minds so that we can place thoughts, pictures and visualizations there to enrich and enhance our life. We start from the premise that the mind holds the key to understanding the deeper meanings of life, and we accept that it has enormous untapped power; so we use meditation as a way of unlocking this power. We can look on this power as the secrets of the mind.

According to many of the ancient philosophies – such as Buddhism, Zen and Yoga – it is definitely possible to reach inwards by using meditation. There are methods of stilling the mind and breathing, of getting physically and mentally relaxed and of adopting certain postures or movements that create a very special rhythm. This defines the invisible pulse that represents the cadence of the inner silent self. Meditation helps us to move into a spiritual awareness of our being. Through it we can harness the higher spirituality of the self to feng shui our hearts and our minds.

What is meditation?

There are many different methods of meditation: some complex and difficult, others refreshingly simple. But every meditation master begins with the need to quiet the mind. Before you start to meditate, it is important for you truly to understand what meditation is. This is because you are dealing with your mind, which transcends your whole persona. You cannot treat your mind frivolously and carelessly, so it is advisable to be quite serious when you start to learn meditation. Here are a few sentences that describe what meditation is. Read each of them slowly and think through these statements. As you do so, your understanding of meditation will expand.

- **Meditation** is the process of holding still and achieving a level of relaxation that slows down the brain waves, bringing our awareness into progressively deeper levels of mind consciousness.

- **Meditation** facilitates transcendence, which helps achieve perfect peace of body, mind and spirit. It engenders subtle feelings of sublime bliss.

- **Meditation** subdues the mind, bringing it to a correct understanding of reality.

- **Meditation** is a gradual process of quietly listening to the mind, transforming it from one level of consciousness to another. It involves one part of the mind observing, analysing and dealing with another part of the mind.

- **Meditation** balances and stabilizes the energy of mind, body and spirit, creating equilibrium of the three aspects of our being.

Because there are so many dimensions to the mind, meditation represents multiple pathways into the inner mind. Contrary to popular misconception, meditation is not simply a matter of sitting in a particular posture or breathing in a particular way.

Meditation has more to do with **the state of one's mind,** *so that while the best results are obtained when one sits quietly in a quiet place, undisturbed and relaxed, one can also meditate while out walking, when working, or when simply resting or lying down.*

Novice practitioners who wish to use meditation to feng shui the inner mind must know from the start how to let go and develop a relaxed state of mind. Anyone wishing to use meditation must first learn how to sit comfortably and think tranquil thoughts. Relaxation facilitates the onset of tranquillity, making it easy to clear the mind of bad energy.

Bad energy always moves fast, and is indicated by a confused mind where thoughts shoot at each other. When thoughts inside your head move with excessive speed, so that visually they resemble bullets and arrows, they signify negative killing chi. When you focus on slowing down your thoughts, you are forcing its chi to meander and flow in a circular motion. The chi of your thoughts then begins to transform into good energy.

Think through this. Whenever you get angry and scold someone, the tendency is to speak much faster than normal. If you watch your words visually, they probably look like bullets and arrows; but if you consciously speak more slowly, you will actually feel yourself softening, thereby blunting your words and eventually losing your anger. So the idea of relaxing the mind is to create and accumulate the dragon's cosmic breath within your heart and your mind, and within your whole body. One of the most effective mediations is to visualize yourself being bathed in a halo of pure white light. This is like being submerged in a cocoon of pure auspicious sheng chi.

Taking a mental bath of pure white light is so exhilarating and auspicious.

I almost always start my meditation sessions by focusing on the relaxation of my physical body and my limbs, the gentle softening of my facial muscles, and a conscious cooling down of tensions and anxieties. I usually close my eyes while I am doing this. Sometimes I play soft soothing music. Other times, when I am feeling spiritual, I chant some mantras.

When I feel completely relaxed, I picture myself surrounded by a bright halo of white light. I think of this white light as the purest energy and I picture myself completely bathed in it. I feel my heart as the core of this light. I feel my body soaking in the white light. I feel my mind becoming crystal clear. Like transparent beautiful crystal. And I stay cocooned and bathed in this white light for as long as I wish ...

I always feel lighter, brighter, happier and more optimistic after that particular meditation. It is a clearing meditation that sweeps away all bad energy and brings in the pure sheng chi. Mental feng shui at its simplest best. I have been doing this meditation for many years, maybe since the early 1980s. No one taught me. I was inspired by something I read about being purified by the bright white light of the sun. Years later when I started learning Buddhist meditation, which is distinctively religious, I discovered to my pleasant surprise that white light visualization was very much a part of the deity visualizations that accompanied the Sadhana meditations.

There are specific postures which can make it easier for the mind to become tranquil and relaxed. It makes sense to learn the special sitting posture when one is first learning how to meditate. This technique facilitates the onset of a calm disposition, the sort that precedes quiet concentration and reduces the mind's susceptibility to distractions.

In many ways of course *meditation is a deeply spiritual practice.* For those of us who simply wish to use it as a tool to feng shui our inner selves and thereby improve our well-being and happiness, our motivation is neither spiritual nor religious. And this is perfectly fine. It is exactly how I started. But because meditation opens the way to a magical transformation of the mind, it is inherently a spiritual process and it can cause a certain spiritual awareness that can take us far beyond our original mundane motivation. So when we use meditation in feng shui, we could well unlock an awakening of our senses that is wholly spiritual.

This is a cause for rejoicing and it can manifest in many different ways. For some this brings heightened sense capabilities – clairvoyance, psychic awakening and so forth. For me it brought a perfectly qualified spiritual teacher. What it brings you reflects your innermost hidden wishes.

If you are not interested in the spiritual and your aspirations are grounded in the material plane alone, your inner mind knows it so you don't need to worry. Your meditation practice is only intended to let you place feng shui symbols and auspicious energies in the crevices and corners of your mind. You will benefit from the absence of killing and poisonous energies inside your body and mind. This means that you will enjoy good health and a happy mental state.

Spiritual awakening will not happen until you indicate that you are ready. Then only will the spiritual seed implanted in your inner mind take root, grow and blossom. So there is never any worry about meditation leading you straight into a spiritual realm of living. You, and you alone, dictate everything that happens or does not happen.

Remember what I said about satisfying the base chakras before you can start to focus on the spiritual upper chakras. Inner feng shui recognizes two planes of inner mind transformation: the happiness that comes from material success, wealth and health at the physical level of existence, and the happiness of a higher spiritual kind. The great thing is that you don't have to worry about the timing. Let your inner mind take care of that. When it is time for your karma to ripen, it will manifest as insight. You will know because you will develop the gift of knowing, what some people refer to as a highly strengthened sixth sense.

Meditation grants access to the inner realm of the mind. When the time is right, it is a process which will generate the experience of insight and this enables us to touch base with our intuition. This may be considered to be a special ability of the spiritual kind.

Intuition is neither feeling nor intellect. It is a higher form of awareness that is spiritual, and it exists in every human individual. Some of us are more spiritually aware than others. Some use this ability consciously and call it their higher wisdom. Some refer to it as the sixth sense. Whatever it is called, intuition is like a soul presence that lives inside the mind. It is therefore spiritual.

Some refer to intuition as the key to the secrets of human happiness. One such person is distinguished Orientalist Dr Paul Brunton, an eminent scholar and noted mystic. Dr Brunton travelled extensively in the Orient, living among yogis, mystics and holy men, and, after a lifetime of study and practice published *The Secret Path* and other best-selling books on comparative religion, mysticism and philosophy. He says:

> **The science of the mind holds the key to man's deepest happiness. There is something within the mind that is neither intellect nor feeling, but more profound than both.**

He calls this the intuition, which he likens to some kind of higher intelligence. In his study of ancient texts unearthed from the Pyramids of Egypt and the temples of the Incas, he compares what he found there with ancient mind practices of Asia. Dr Brunton also searched for surviving practitioners of genuine Oriental wisdom and magic.

So he travelled deep into their worlds to witness the mind marvels performed by the yogi magicians of high mountains of India, to meet with the Sufi mystics of old Persia and to observe the fantastic feats of endurance exhibited by the high lamas of Tibet and Nepal. He saw these holy men demonstrate control over what are considered the involuntary muscles of their body, change their physical temperature, and perform seemingly magical feats of endurance, simply by using the mind. This convinced him of the existence of a higher energy inside the human mind, energy he termed intuition. Dr Brunton investigated their methods of awakening intuition.

'When the reasoning, thinking intellect subsides its activity,' he wrote, 'intuition has a clear field in which to manifest itself. Hence the necessity to tame the mind and tame the constant, ceaseless activity of the intellect.'

What he is describing is the practice of meditation – the process of subduing the mind and bringing it to a level of tranquillity where deeper more powerful energies begin to emerge. With this energy coming through, the inner consciousness comes into focused awareness. This is when realizations of the spiritual kind take place. A *realization* is a sudden inspiring thought that defines some profound truth. It comes suddenly like a laser beam, sharp, stunning and awesome. It lights up your world, if only for an instant, and your understanding of life is suddenly very clear.

Attaining realizations of insights is a moment of rare bliss.

It is like receiving a mountain of blessings, so magical is its effect

and so awesome is its power suddenly to make everything

clear to you.

These brilliant realizations seem to come into the mind from nowhere. This is one of the most astounding results of deep meditation: realizations that represent solutions to daily problems, or offer penetrating insights into the meaning of existence or encourage the flow of seemingly magical mental activity. Attaining these realizations is one of the prime goals of the practice of meditative inner feng shui, and they usually show themselves when they are least expected.

There are three types of meditation, which are useful when working on inner feng shui. These are meditations for stabilizing the chi of the body and mind; meditations for activating the flow of chi in the body and mind; and meditations for visualizing the chi in the inner mind.

Stabilizing the chi of body and mind

These meditations achieve mental quiet, tranquillity and inner calm. They create balance and a state of harmony. Some refer to it as the single pointed concentration method whereby mental tranquillity is achieved by concentrating on one object – *the human breath*. The motivation behind this meditative technique is to create a completely balanced body and mind so that chi flows smoothly and unimpeded. The method here is to capture the exclusive attention of the mind by focusing it pointedly on the human breath. When wandering thoughts distract the mind and its attention wavers, the concentration is gently but firmly brought back to focus on the breath.

To ensure that the concentration stays undisturbed, outside distractions should be kept to a minimum. Meditate in a cool, quiet room: disturbances and interruptions should be firmly locked out. Don't expect to be able to attain perfect concentration overnight. It is an extremely hard thing to achieve because the mind is so very difficult to subdue.

Start by consciously relaxing the physical body.

Limb by limb, body part by body part, flex with tension, and then let go. Do this slowly up and down your body until you feel yourself sink heavily into yourself. Try not to doze off.

Don't worry if you do fall asleep. I almost always get so relaxed I simply fall asleep, but when I succeed in keeping awake, what the inner mind triggers off for me is simply sensational. So let this inspire you. The tendency to sleep can be overcome if you keep your eyes open when you meditate, and if you sit rather than lie down.

Relaxed concentration is so important that without it the meditation process becomes ineffective. The tough part is achieving relaxation without dozing off. This comes after some practice and the mind succeeds in staying quiet for longer and longer periods.

Now focus in on the human breath.

Without the least bit of strain, watch your breath as it goes in and out of your body. Breathe in through your nose, slowly and calmly, deeply and fully. Feel the breath go deep inside you and follow it as it goes deep into your abdomen. Then feel it come out again. Once more, it moves slowly and gently.

You should neither force the breath nor hold it until you feel uncomfortable. The goal here is not to breathe as deeply or as slowly as you can. That is a far more advanced method, which we do not yet need. The goal is simply to follow the breath. This is an exercise in developing mental one-pointed concentration. This requires practice. I have already alerted you to the possibility of falling asleep. Another obstacle is when your mind starts to wander, or become distracted with mindless chatter. When this happens, gently bring the mind back to the breath again. Keep bringing your attention back to the breath.

In the beginning do this exercise for ten minutes. Do not sit and meditate for long periods of time during the early days. Better to do it often and regularly than to practise it in fits and starts of intense enthusiasm followed by long periods of complete avoidance. Meditation brings the best results when you do it regularly each day or three times a week, even if it is only for 15 minutes each time.

The Tao – a state of perfectly stabilized chi

When you come close to attaining focused and single-pointed concentration, you know you are making progress. Concentration is one of the hardest skills to master but once you have it, mental strength and agility open up an inner world that is beyond description. The fully stabilized consciousness is described by meditation masters as a state of such perfect harmony that balance of the Tao is achieved. This symbolizes the perfect union of yin chi with yang chi. Yin and yang are the two poles of the cosmic spectrum of existence.

This is when, it is said, the mind realizes the invisible entity described as the transcended mind. It is a very special state of mind, rather like being spaced out, floating yet mentally alert and aware... and all around there is nothing. There is probably no way you can attain this level by yourself. For such advanced realizations you must have a qualified teacher. Advanced meditation requires secret techniques and methods and the chanting of certain mantras to open up inner doorways. So when you read about these levels of attainment you should know the difference between that and what we are doing. Highly advanced meditative attainments are for yogis. Don't be anxious or in a hurry to learn such techniques until you are ready.

The best advice I can give you is to go with the flow. Have a good and correct motivation and then let what you do to enhance and energize the feng shui of your body and your mind bring enjoyment into your world. Let your practice of feng shui be a journey into the boundless, but also enjoy your life and be happy as you progress.

Remember that you are not perfect. You cannot become perfect without years and years of practice. Being able to meditate is not the same as becoming a master at it. It takes the yogics a whole lifetime to master the practices of yoga and meditation.

Starting with simple breathing meditation enables you to stabilize and access the inner mind and this is already an achievement. It is good enough for our purpose. When the mind is stabilized, the chi inside the body and mind and along the spiritual meridians of the body will flow unencumbered at a pace that is harmonious and auspicious. It is amazing how powerful are the effects of having a stable inner field of chi.

Breathing always creates a rhythm when the mind follows its flow in and out of the body. It is lighting the pathways and making certain that a precious balance of yin and yang chi is nicely maintained. Your mind and body become centred because your inner mind is centred and properly balanced.

Each time you do this meditation exercise, spend some time feeling the inner cadence and rhythm of your being. It is a very beautiful feeling. Savour it in consonance with the quiet beating of your heart, the sense of lightness that makes you truly appreciate your life. It is the ultimate positive feeling, and it attracts such good fortune. The peerless light within is internalized in your heart. You feel centred and very grounded.

There are many feng shui visualizations you can start to practise once you reach this level of stable chi consciousness. Try to be constant in your efforts at attaining a heightened state of awareness. Practise as regularly as you can, and when you have become reasonably confident that you have succeeded in creating a state of stabilized chi, then program your mind to recognize this state of consciousness. Snap your fingers, or raise your third finger – devise a signal, which the mind recognizes as the trigger for reaching this state. This is a semi-hypnotic suggestion which acts as a secret password or signal to let your mind know each time you wish to be in this state. At this alpha level of consciousness, the inner mind is very attuned to thought suggestions. Programming the mind this way makes daily stabilizing chi meditations a lot easier. Centring the body and mind on a daily basis creates a level of equanimity that is itself very calming. When you go further into the feng shui visualization exercises of the next chapter, the simple phenomenon of a happy thought here can be magnified a million times.

Activating the flow of chi

This meditation introduces the energy centres of the body and contains the five elements of creative and intellectual thought within the mind. Here the focus is on activating the flow of chi inside the body and mind using thought consciousness. When you develop the capability of using your own thoughts you can move the chi within your body and your mind simply by using your thoughts. This exercise will familiarize you further with the power of thought energy.

So, think strongly that you can get the cosmic chi to move according to the flow of your breath. This is called the *flow of chi consciousness*. Breath meditation enables you to follow the breath. Now you start to watch this flow of breath, observing it closely, especially the way it moves, the way it stops and the way it lingers. When you become comfortable with this movement of chi, introduce white light into the flow.

Think, as you breathe in, that the pure cosmic chi of the universe is entering your body as pure white light.

Picture this as a flow of fluorescent light moving alongside your breath and lighting up your body, in the process leaving precious atoms of good fortune along this main flow of chi inside you. Then when you breathe out look closely at the same white light and imagine it has picked up traces of black ink, soot and dirt from your body. As you breathe out, these negatives are expelled from the body.

Do this very important meditation exercise for at least a week before moving on to the next level of energizing the flow of chi. If you have a hard time thinking of white light, look at a bright light bulb for a few seconds, then close your eyes and you will see the light right in front of you even when your eyes are closed, such is the power of light. You will discover, as we move into the techniques of inner feng shui exercises, that *lights play a crucial role in activating the inner chi*. Different coloured lights can be incorporated into the meditation to raise the different elements of the chakras – water, wood, fire, earth and metal – but the most powerful is white light because white light amalgamates all the colours of the universe. White light is also the purest form of chi.

The Indians have taken chakra-raising meditations (also called *kundalini* meditations) to fantastically high levels and what we are doing here is only a very simple method of engaging the chakras. Start by identifying the chakra points along the central axis of your body (see the illustration shown here). Study the energy points and commit them to memory.

Chakra points

7. Spiritual (crown)
6. Intuitive
5. Creative
4. Heart
3. Power
2. Sensation
1. Survival
   (base of spine)

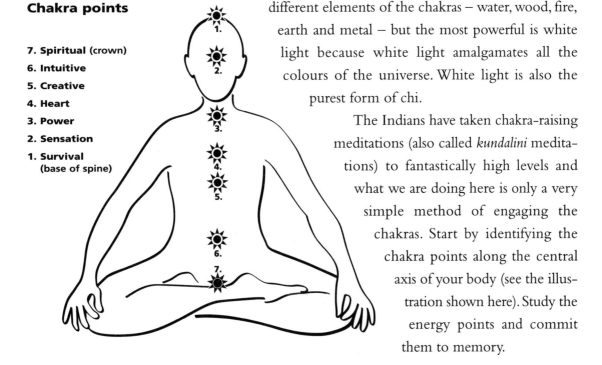

The base chakras

1. At the base is the root chakra. Think of it as red light.
2. Above that is the lower abdomen chakra – orange light.
3. Above is the solar plexus chakra – golden yellow light.

The three base chakras are of the fire and earth elements. They symbolize the concentrations of energy that govern the material enjoyments of the body. When we think of wealth, food, sex and gratification of these sense enjoyments we think of these three base chakras. If this is what you wish for very much and your practice of inner feng shui is focused on getting and accumulating these material enjoyments, then you must focus on the flow of chi moving strongly in these three areas.

> Think of the three base chakras as intensely coloured lights, red for the root chakra, orange for the next one and yellow for the next. These are yang earthly colours. Now think of a bright white line joining these three centres. And finally think of the white light as flowing up and down joining the three centres, then think of the flow going round these centres in a clockwise direction. Let the flow of white light move slowly and gently. Imagine your energy centres being enhanced by this flow of light. Think that what is happening here is the chi flowing auspiciously round and through your chi centres that govern your material well-being. This activates satisfaction of these centres, bringing material good fortune your way. Please do this exercise with a positive and happy mind.

When you focus your concentration on the base chakras, it activates the flow of chi within your body that is related to all the material and sense pleasures that many of us want. Much of conventional feng shui, in fact all of it, has to do with attracting energy which brings the abundance of material pleasures. Thus wanting wealth, a good career, success, fame, family, love, sex, descendants and health – all of these aspirations represent the satisfaction of the three base chakras.

Your practice of conventional spatial and time feng shui can be strongly enhanced by inner feng shui meditations that energize the auspicious flow of chi. More: if you want your material well-being to be capped by the growth of spiritual awareness, you can move on to engage the four upper chakras.

The upper chakras

4. The heart chakra – green light and a 12-petalled lotus
5. The throat chakra – blue light and a 16-petalled lotus
6. The third eye chakra – lilac and a 96-petalled lotus
7. The crown chakra – violet or white and a 1,000-petalled lotus

Meditations that involve all seven chakras are extremely powerful in balancing the inner chi of both the body and the mind. The benefits transcend both material and spiritual abundance.

Follow the flow of chi from the crown chakra all the way down to the root chakra and then up again in a slow circular flow that is made up of white light, and that joins up all the energy centres. Visualize all the seven energy points lighted up in the colours indicated, from red at the base root chakra to orange to yellow to green to blue to lilac and violet culminating in white at the top of the crown chakra – and then down again. When you think of the light moving upwards let the light be in the front part of the body and when you follow the flow of chi downwards let the light be at the back of the body.

When you get to be really good at this visualization, you can create many circular flows of lights that embrace and cocoon your whole body until you become an entity of bright white light. All seven of your chakras are lighted up like coloured bulbs.

> Picture your body and mind surrounded by white light. Keep the chi flowing harmoniously and energizing you. Concentrate on this for a little while and then slowly dim the lights one by one... Do not come out of this meditation suddenly. Just before coming out of it think through your motivation for doing that particular meditation. This will reinforce your intention of activating chi for material and spiritual abundance in your life.

Ideally, chi should never flow in a tense or anxious manner, so all through your meditation sessions, never allow your thoughts to become tense or anxious. Always sit comfortably. Each time a negative thought comes into your mind, gently push it away. Do not dwell on negative thoughts about events or people, as this gives them energy. Just imagine these thoughts being swept and transformed by the powerful white light that moves from one chakra point to another.

Visualizing the chi

This meditation engages the powerful eye chakra, which many people now refer to as the third eye. This concentration of energy lies between the eyes on the forehead. When the flow of energy here is in a state of harmony, the individual experiences a heightened state of awareness that manifests in enhanced intuition. Inner awareness becomes extremely powerful because this awareness connects to the material and universal world. When the energy flow here is unbalanced and in disarray the individual simply cannot awaken the spiritual side. What is perceived will lack the special 'seeing' of the inner eye. Intuition cannot awaken, and progress into inner understanding is blocked.

When the inner seeing eye gets blocked, mental and meditative visualizations lack power; in fact it will become extremely difficult to move on to the next stage, which involves the creation of images in the mind. Meditative visualizations are the highest form of meditation. They are also the most potent.

Start by calming the mind and making yourself feel centred and very relaxed. Generate the correct motivation, which is that you want to create a balanced and harmonious flow of chi in your eye chakra to facilitate the development of your powers of visualization. Then think of a gentle lilac light between your eyes. Stay with this light for a while. Think that this is your inner eye and that it is opening to let you see things that you would not normally see. Stay very calm.

Think of a lilac-coloured lotus with many petals in the middle of the lilac light. This is a 96-petalled lotus, and inside the lotus is a sparkling gemstone that reflects everything in the universe. Try to stay with this picture and imagine the light from this eye chakra glowing and throbbing in between your eyes.

Next slowly imagine the flow of light moving around the lotus and jewel in a clockwise direction. This is the yin energy moving. It is the female energy. Next imagine the flow of light moving in an anticlockwise direction. This is the yang energy moving and it is the male energy. When you have stabilized the energy of your eye chakra flowing harmoniously, dedicate this harmonious flow to successful visualizations.

Try to do this exercise at least once a week. With practice it will greatly enhance your success in doing meditative visualization. Control of this ability will give you excellent control over your mind, and by extension, over your mankind luck. The more firmly you establish the desired goal of your meditation session, the stronger will be your motivation, and the higher your chances of success.

Start by making the achievement of relaxation and the calming of your mind the immediate short-term goal of your meditation. Later as you become more adept at the practice you can start to get more ambitious and meditate on subduing your mind, programming it to overcome the three poisons, and then programming it to become receptive to good fortune. From there your motivation can make a definite shift into more spiritual realms (if you so wish) when you start to contemplate more profound concepts of life, like the true nature of reality. Or you can stay firmly in the physical plane where your goals relate to material good fortune. Whatever your ultimate aspirations, note that in the beginning you should aim merely to subdue the mind, stabilize it and gently push negative thoughts out of your system.

Feng shui for your meditation place

It is always a good idea to set aside a special room for meditation and this should be a quiet place, where you will not be disturbed. It does not matter where this room is except that it should not be directly above or below a kitchen, a toilet or a heavy piece of furniture. The room is better if it is in the back half of the home.

If you wish, you can meditate in front of an altar. Whatever your religion, meditating in the presence of an object of faith or a holy object such as a statue of Jesus Christ or of Buddha has a particularly calming effect on the mind. If you have an altar, make sure that the altar is not sharing a wall with a toilet or has a toilet directly above. The altar should also not be directly facing the door. If it is, when you meditate make sure the altar and not the door is behind you. Never meditate with your back to the door as this is most unfavourable.

The room should have a comfortable temperature level. If you like, you can have a special cushion or chair to aid in your meditation. Let the décor be quietly soothing. There are no rules on colours except that red is not a good colour for a meditation room. Make sure that you sit facing one of your auspicious directions when you meditate. This will ensure that the chi that comes towards you as you sit in meditation is auspicious. Do not sit facing a direction that brings killing energy towards you. Apply the Kua formula of the 8 Mansions school of feng shui when preparing your meditation room (see pp. 163–4).

The meditation cushion

Before you start, take your time to find a meditation cushion that feels right. If you are not used to sitting cross-legged (let alone attempting the more difficult lotus pose) I suggest you get a cushion that is hard and at least three inches high. This will make it a lot easier for you.

When you first start using the cushion, place some long-stemmed grass under it. It is believed that if you then place this same grass under your pillow when you sleep at night, you will have a meaningful dream. You need do this only for the first meditation session. The best colours for meditation cushions are yellow, maroon or earth colours. You want to sit on an earth element to create a feeling of being well centred and grounded. I recommend you not to use black or blue cushions: you will be sitting on the water element, which is unstable. It is a good idea to use the same meditation cushion for all your sessions.

Posture

Because of the interdependence of the mind and the physical body, a correct sitting posture is encouraged. There are seven points to remember:

1. **Legs** Master practitioners recommend sitting in the full lotus position, i.e. with the feet placed, sole upwards, on the thigh of the other leg. This is supposedly the preferred posture of practising Buddhists and Hindu wise men. Indeed, most statues and pictures of the seated Buddha indicate the lotus position. In reality of course the lotus posture is very difficult, and for many people even

impossible; so if you like, you can sit in the half-lotus posture, where only one foot is resting on the thigh of the opposite leg, and the other foot is resting on the floor in front.

I have always meditated sitting cross-legged with both feet on the floor. I find that when I place a firm cushion under the buttocks it helps to keep my back straight, and reduces the pins and needles effect. The straight back is vitally important in getting the most out of your session because it facilitates the flow of chi. If this posture is difficult for you, you can sit on a straight-backed chair with both feet planted firmly on the floor. This is the Egyptian posture. In old pictures of the Egyptians they are shown seated in this way. If even this is difficult, try lying down with your back straight and your hands by your sides. This position is also acceptable. The drawback is that you will find yourself falling asleep all too quickly!

2. **Arms** Shoulders and arms should be relaxed. Arms should not be pressed against the body, but held a little away. This improves circulation and assists in keeping you awake. Rest your hands lightly on your knees, palm downwards, or hold them loosely on your lap with fingers aligned. There are different hand positions, what the Buddhists refer to as *mudras*, and I have been told that joining the thumbs pointing upwards aids concentration. If you want to feel the chi, you place your palms facing each other one above the other. Imagine the chi or energy lying between your hands. After a while the hands begin to warm up and tingle. When this happens, feel the chi flowing up your arms and all through your body. You can imagine the chi as a white light or as a pure force that energizes you. Whenever your hands tire you can change your hand *mudra*.

3. **Back** This is the most vital part of your posture. The back must be straight, held totally relaxed but upright. It is only when the back is straight that energy can flow easily and naturally through it. Also, a straight back is conducive to longer periods of meditation. I have found that it is only when I am comfortably upright that I

can feel my mind relaxing and letting go. So if at first you find it difficult to stay upright, make an effort to get it correct before proceeding further.

4. **Eyes** I prefer to meditate with my eyes lightly closed. This enables me to shut out distractions and also makes it easier for me to relax and to visualize. It is not however advisable to keep the eyes too tightly shut. Indeed, many masters advise that the eyes be kept lightly open, but cast downwards. They say that closing the eyes makes for drowsiness and the advent of dream images – which some claim hinder true meditation. I would say that you should do whatever makes you feel comfortable.

5. **Mouth** Your entire mouth and jaw should be relaxed and should hang loose. Teeth are kept slightly apart, with the lips kept lightly together.

6. **Tongue** The tongue should be held slightly touching the upper palate behind the teeth. This stops the saliva from flowing, but more important, enables you to meditate for a longer period without feeling discomfort.

7. **Head** This should be held naturally balanced. Do not tilt the head either too far forward or too far backwards. Hold it so that your gaze can be directed naturally towards the floor in front of you. If the head position is too high or too low, it encourages wandering thoughts, thereby hindering the meditation.

If you find the above guidelines on posture a little tedious to follow, start by simply sitting cross-legged and making yourself thoroughly comfortable and relaxed. It is vital that your mind is not stressed by worries about posture. Far better to get it slightly wrong and be totally calm and relaxed than to get it totally right but be full of tension. In meditation, success depends so much on the ability to relax.

Establish regularity of practice. This is necessary if you wish to experience the benefits of meditation. You can succeed in stilling the mind only when you are determined to practise regularly. At first, set aside a few minutes each day – perhaps 20 to 30 minutes early in the morning or late at night. Do this every day, or at least three times a week. If you go for weeks (or, worse, months) without practising, you cannot achieve the kind of mind stabilizing you are hoping for.

Each time you start again, you are back to square one. To make progress, try to meditate at least once a day. No matter if you are tired, really stressed and not in the mood to do so – make the effort to sit quietly for a few minutes anyway. Try to discipline yourself. Believe me, if you start to practise regularly for a week you will already feel the benefits. You actually become happier and feel luckier. This is what I often describe as the magic of the mind.

Meditating to music

Many people find soothing music very helpful to get into a relaxed frame of mind. If you are one of them, you can play music very softly in the background. My way of getting started is to strike my singing bowl, close my eyes slightly and follow the sound until it recedes. The sound takes me into the deeper recesses of my mind ...

Personally I prefer the single sharp piercing note of the singing bowl because by the time the sound fades away I have entered into my inner consciousness. I find that music keeps me in the outer environment. But I know many people who have used relaxing music with great success. Use whatever works for you.

If you want to try the singing bowl, make certain that you get one which has been fired from seven types of metal including gold and silver. This is what gives the bowl such a beautiful sound.

Keep early sessions short

When you first start to meditate it is best if the sessions last no more than 20 minutes. You can meditate for 10 minutes and still feel the benefits. Try to end your sessions when your mind and body are still fresh. Do not tire yourself out, or force yourself to meditate to the extent that your feet or legs hurt from being in one position for too long. Let the sessions grow in length slowly. Your mind should also come out of the session eager for more, rather than relieved it is over. Do remember that coercion of any kind makes you vulnerable to frustration.

Stay physically relaxed

In your meditation session, wear loose clothing which does not impede your internal circulation, and feel clean and cool. Make sure the temperature is neither too hot nor too cold. In short, stay really comfortable. Later, when you have become more expert at the practice and have learnt not to be distracted by physical discomforts, you will become immune to these superficialities. But until then, it is a good idea to help you become relaxed. Physical relaxation can be facilitated by the practice of such disciplines as t'ai chi and yoga, or other chi qong exercise. In fact any method that eases physical tensions and moves the flow of chi can be incorporated into the meditation session.

Also stay mentally relaxed

This calls for you consciously to let go of worries, problems and all involvement with the outside world. Instead, focus on the silence and quiet of the inner world. It helps to recall soothing moments of tranquillity experienced in the immediate past. Remembering these occasions makes the process of achieving mental relaxation easier. Sometimes it helps if gentle, soothing music is played softly in the background. Rhythmic sounds help the mind to ease into a state of tranquillity. Whatever works for you can be incorporated into your personal programme.

Stay alert

Do not fall asleep, although if you do doze off during the initial stages you should not be alarmed or in any way discouraged. In the process of relaxing your mind and body, it is easy for the mind to enter too quickly into other levels of consciousness and if you are not used to staying awake and alert at these levels of consciousness you will fall asleep! If this happens, simply persevere. Don't close your eyes while meditating, and don't meditate lying down.

Be prepared for occasional setbacks

Do not have high expectations from your early sessions. If you try too hard it may hinder your progress. Allow the mind to relax and let your thought flow at its own pace. Let it take you where it will. Be a passive observer. Be prepared for anything, but do not be unduly disturbed by whatever happens.

Watch your different moods as they manifest over several sessions of meditation. Some days will be better than other days. Plus, genuine valuable results – the experience of insight, of total relaxation, of focused concentration – all take time to achieve. Go easy on yourself.

It is advisable to have a teacher

It is to be expected that if you have someone more experienced than you, or, better yet, a master to guide you in your meditation sessions, your progress will be much faster. But it is not easy to find a qualified teacher whose schedule fits neatly into yours. Besides, it is better *not* to have a teacher unless you can find someone you genuinely have a great deal of respect for, and with whom you can communicate comfortably and with confidence. It sometimes takes years before you come across someone suitable, and I often tell my friends not to get too stressed about this – when the time is right you will find that a master materializes in your life with no effort at all on your part.

Please believe me and don't get stressed about this. The worst thing is to take on just anybody. It could do a lot of harm if the person whom you take as a teacher is not skilful enough, and guides you wrongly. If you do not have a teacher, rely on your higher wisdom to guide you.

If you practise regularly there is no reason why you should not make progress. It is the same with the practice of conventional feng shui. How many times have I had to write to reassure my readers that they can do feng shui themselves, that they do not need to bring in a consultant who is not qualified! If you take on such a teacher you will be doing yourself a grave injustice. So be relaxed about this.

Feel satisfied about the fact that you are making an effort to meditate, and to transform your mind. The very act of doing this is itself a form of meditation. The act of tuning inwards to listen to your subconscious inner mind is meditation. Just do the simple mental programming exercises and breathing meditations and then proceed to work with the empowering feng shui exercises and workshops (see pp. 161–87). You need not become a meditation expert to harvest all the benefits of inner feng shui practice.

Practise in a private place

Practising feng shui for the mind should be something very private. Your present environment can be as peaceful as a lazy summer's day on a mountainside or as busy and loud as the back room of a cramped city shop. More realistically, it will be your bedroom where you can enjoy all the privacy in the world. It does not matter where your place of practice is, but you should be able to consider it as private. You must be able to switch into yourself without being distracted.

I always recommend that the first mental exercise to do is to practise mentally switching out of your physical environment. Do this so well that you have the ability to switch out instantly. You can do this with any of the methods of *inner mind focus* contained in this book. Everything you need can also be actualized by your mind *inside your mind*. This is referred to as *mental visualization* – the art of creating real pictures inside you. Such a technique can be mastered very easily and quickly if you use the right methods. I believe that all of us carry these skills inside us and it only requires a catalyst for us to unlock them. Reading this book is itself such a catalyst. It is likely that your time to discover your own dragon magic has ripened, and that you are ready to start unlocking the chi within you!

Do not involve others in your practice

You will find that the practice of inner mind awareness and transformation brings with it a whole range of super-abilities. It works differently for different people. So when you feel yourself being blessed with special abilities, at first these may seem strange and magical. You may even feel you are becoming psychic and clairvoyant. If you notice these abilities arising inside you, do not talk about them.

Just acknowledge them quietly and make a silent commitment to use your new skills to contribute to the greater good of your world. Never talk about any of the awareness and perceptions that come to you. Let all and every insight you gain stay secret. Keep silent. Let them be part of your own private inner world.

When you talk about any of the beautiful insights with others, you are taking the risk of introducing negative poison that will set you back. And do not be too anxious: you must learn to let go and take a very easygoing and relaxed attitude. It is not necessary to have blind faith in the practice, but don't weaken yourself with harmful negative vibrations. These cause blocks in the flow of energy, thereby impeding your progress.

The learning process should be at your own pace. Move up the learning curve at whatever speed you wish. Practise intensely every day, or let it be a weekend thing. There is no need to rush. Your practice should be structured according to your schedule of life and work. You must be convinced that the methods and tools of feng shui for the mind are working for *you*. You must feel confident that you are benefiting from the practice.

Meditations should not require drastic changes to your lifestyle

Remember that meditation is not an external activity. It is internal, involving the transformation of the way you think. Meditation will make you more sensitive, and improve the clarity with which you view your world. Day-to-day routines will reveal fresh new insights. But changes to your behaviour patterns will be subtle. They will also be very deep so that over time you find these changes creeping over you rather than suddenly overwhelming you. A perceptible calmness will slowly but surely take hold in your life. It is quite a beautiful experience, and when you begin to feel it, keep at it. Do not stop, because when you do, each time you forget to meditate for a few weeks, you will find that you have to start all over again.

Do not give up

The experience of insight and the meditative response from your inner mind must never be taken for granted. They can prove to be elusive, and frustratingly just out of reach. So do stay centred and quietly determined to keep pursuing the practice. The benefits are real and very tangible. Do not give up. Even when you have progressed to doing visualizations and become really expert in feng shui-ing your body and mind, keep doing these meditation sessions.

Coping with problems of meditation

When you first start to meditate, you will meet up with some difficulties experienced by most beginners. Do not feel discouraged.

Mental restlessness and distractions

This is perhaps the most common difficulty encountered at every stage of meditation. The mind is naturally restless, and it tends to wander from subject to subject. It is wild and undisciplined and changeable. From nowhere will come unconnected thoughts, recollections and remembrances. These wandering thoughts reflect the surface of the mind, and in order to feel the benefits of meditation we need to penetrate the surface and enter into the inner depths of the mind. So when thoughts enter into the mind, it is vital not to get excited or to panic. Or even to feel irritated. Just keep pushing these thoughts out of the mind. Do it consciously, bringing the concentration back to either the white light or the breath again and again.

Make the mind stay calm; let the natural rhythm of

breathing engage your attention as totally as possible.
Observe any wandering thoughts that enter without
actually getting involved. Tell yourself they are like waves
in your mind, ebbing and flowing. Acknowledge them
but ignore them as well. Keep making the effort to stay
in control of your mind, and over your thoughts.

If the mental restlessness persists, check your posture. Make sure your spine
is straight and your head is tilted slightly forward. The mind tends to get
distracted more easily when the head is placed too high. Diffusing the
room light also helps, since brightness excites the senses causing the mind
to get restless. Patience is essential when dealing with a restless mind.
Never lose patience. Just work at gently pushing out all thoughts that
enter. In time you will see results.

Physical discomfort

While it is easy enough to say 'Stay relaxed and comfortable', in practice
this is not so easy to achieve. A great deal of discomfort is felt, most of it
caused by the mind. Many of these mind-related feelings – worries, fears,
distractions, anger, unresolved irritations – can affect the meditation
session, causing physical irritations that block the smooth flow of concentration.

Gradually focus your attention on every part of your
body, systematically starting from the tips of your toes,
and working your way slowly upwards. This conscious
body relaxation method will help ease tensions in various
parts of the body, and also assist in taking away
attention from whatever may be worrying your mind.

Taking slow and deep breaths also helps to alleviate physical discomfort.

Concentrate on slightly lengthening the out-breath, i.e. slowly drawing it out. This makes your body relax. If you like, you can supplement it with a wonderful visualization. As you breathe in, picture a stream of white light entering your body, filling it with lightness, and as you breathe out picture yourself breathing out any tension or stress that is disturbing you. Do this for a few moments and you will begin to feel better.

If your posture is causing you discomfort, it is OK to shift slightly, or change your position. Remember that meditation is an activity of the mind, and while it is recommended to stay quite still when you are meditating, it is perfectly acceptable for you to move your joints occasionally if it makes you feel better.

If you are feeling real pain in some part of your body, try at first to bear the pain. Use the mind to focus in on it, but transform the perception of pain into another form of energy. Tell yourself it is not pain, that it is just a new sensation. Then observe the way your mind reacts to your new perception and see if you can use your mind to control your physical reactions. If you cannot and the pain persists, then change position. If you succeed in transcending the pain, give yourself a pat on the back, because this means you have achieved something fantastic with your mind.

It is also possible to use the mind to transfer the pain from one part of the physical body to another: if you have a headache you can transfer the pain in the head on to, say, your legs. You can actually use your mind to reduce the pain. Picture the pain disappearing. Use the white light for this experiment. Picture the white engulfing the pain and eating it until there is no pain left!

Getting sleepy

This is just the opposite of a mind that is too active. Sometimes if you start your meditation session at the end of the day, you may be so physically exhausted that getting into a relaxed state just sends you to sleep. Usually this happens because your posture is more conducive to sleep than to meditation, so do check this. At any rate, if you are very exhausted, it is better for you to go to sleep instead of trying to fight the exhaustion.

If, however, sleepiness is a real problem each time you try to meditate, I suggest you change the time of your meditation sessions. Have a warm bath before starting, and sit with your back very straight and your eyes open. Do not close your eyes; just keep them downcast and relaxed. If the sleepiness continues, take a break of a week or two before trying again.

Strange experiences

When I first started meditating many years ago, I had a terrible fright. In the middle of one of my sessions I was disturbed by what a master later told me was a manifestation of an inner fear. This so-called inner fear manifested in the image of a very ugly monster, and it was *not* pleasant! I stopped meditating for months after that.

I later discovered that strange experiences and unusual images do occasionally happen. There is no need to worry. These are not ghosts or spirits. Sometimes you can even feel yourself falling off the edge of a cliff, or being chased by someone or something terrifying. If this happens to you, stay very calm. There is truly nothing to worry about. It is just your mind adjusting to the new mental activity. Even when you are disturbed by monstrous images, just tell yourself that they are the manifestation of inner, deeper fears. Use the opportunity to *confront* these images and cure yourself of some hidden phobia. Acknowledge your fears and you will overcome them. This is how I overcame my fear of the dark, my fear of ghosts and spirits and all the fantasy creatures of the night – the horrible faces that were a heritage of my childhood days; pictures of Frankenstein's monster and Dracula and the Pontianak (a Malayan vampire) impressed on to my subconscious mind from seeing all those movies. That is why to this day I do not allow my daughter to see horror movies! When you meditate you are in effect attempting to unlock the images of your subconscious mind. So do not be unduly alarmed if occasionally you *see* something frightening. If such images persist, discontinue the meditation for a while, or if you have a master consult him.

Feelings of depression

One of the common side effects of meditation for beginners is that sometimes they are overcome by unexplained feelings of depression, negativity and discouragement. If you find that this is happening to you, it is symptomatic of a mind that is deeply imbued with very negative thoughts. The act of meditating allows many of these to surface. You must work at it. Acknowledge the negatives. Let them arise. Acknowledge the feelings of depression and try to discover the real reasons for them. Releasing a long-buried traumatic event or experience is often one of the best ways of becoming free of it.

Meditation is a means of purifying the mind. When you are attempting to clean out mind negatives, it is like washing clothes. The dirtier the stains, the dirtier will be the initial water that is used to do the cleaning. But after a while, when all the stains of negativity have been cleansed out, you will begin to feel much better. There will be a feeling of lightness and liberation.

Finally, do not expect results too quickly. There is no normal average length of time it takes. Meditation is a deeply personal exercise and every individual will experience subtle differences. Have faith and confidence in yourself. In time the feelings of depression will be replaced by other more worthwhile feelings of self-worth and confidence. This is the ultimate objective. So keep at it.

6.

Visualization techniques

Creating pictures in the mind during meditation, or when you are lying down relaxed, is the most amazingly easy way of enhancing your feng shui and actualizing wishes into reality. This is an exciting 'secret of the mind' that I have used with great success for many years now.

isualization has become a popular and integral part of New Age consciousness. This reflects growing global awareness of the mind's extra dimensions, and as the old century drew to a close, more attention was focused on investigating its immense potential. The New Age movement in the United States and in Europe has turned to Eastern traditions in search of meditative and spiritual practices that can help tap into the mind's potential.

The Chinese have used meditation techniques for almost all and every kind of human endeavour. Basically, meditation is used to raise the internal chi of the body and mind. It is incorporated in all the Chinese exercises, like kung fu and chi kung; it is part of the curriculum in the study of calligraphy, painting, cooking and in the passing of the imperial exams. Meditation is, above all, an integral part of those skills engaged in the profession of divination.

So you should not be surprised when you discover that most master calligraphers, kung fu artists, or feng shui experts are usually also master practitioners of the art of meditation. Anyone who excels in their field of expertise will at some stage of their life have learnt how to meditate. I am almost certain that many of China's elderly leaders do some serious meditation each day. Certainly, many of the tycoons of China, Hong Kong, Taiwan and Singapore incorporate reflective meditation into their daily routines.

Almost every meditation technique and method used by the Chinese employs powerful visualizations. Mental imaging of pictures has always played a central part in Chinese techniques of meditation but for a very long time this was a closely guarded secret. Only those who made the study of these matters their life's work were taught how to incorporate the breath and mind pictures into their daily workouts and practices. In this century, however, a great deal of these visualization techniques and scenarios – many involving the use of feng shui symbols and good fortune images – have become public so that these secrets really are not secrets any more.

This rich imagery has been captured on celluloid. Those of you who have seen the costume dramas made by the film industries of Hong Kong and Taiwan know what I am referring to. These productions have transformed ancient classical tales into lavishly costumed films. In them we see images of people flying, white light transforming into a kaleidoscope of stunning images, fairies that bring good fortune, meditating holy men who use their chi to create extraordinary magic and feats that defy the imagination. I have to confess that I am an ardent fan of these stunning movies and have been for many years. With the discovery of computer graphics, the images of visualization transmitted via the movie screen have improved so much they simply take my breath away. Certainly they are a match for George Lucas's *Star Wars*! When you see these images in full colour on the screen, you will find that your own mental visualization gets a lot easier. This is because a picture, once seen, stays imprinted in the mind.

Visualizations are contained in many of the 'secret' meditative and prayer practices of Buddhism, Taoism and Hinduism in all their different traditions. I am told that many of these visualizations are very ritualistic in that they follow a script of some kind (in Buddhism these scripts are prayers called sadhanas) which describes what is to be visualized in great detail; often these visualizations are helped along by the playing of musical instruments and the chanting of mantras. Obviously in religious practices the visualized image is often of a deity which has meaning to the practitioner.

Taoist deities (which are very feng shui significant) often reflect material aspirations. Thus there are the various gods of wealth, the god of longevity, the three star gods and so forth. *Buddhist deities* include the Buddha of Compassion, the Buddha of Loving-Kindness and the Buddha of Wisdom.

Visualization in feng shui

Visualization also plays a very big part in the successful practice of feng shui. The feng shui masters I have met and for whom I have great respect are experts in the practice of meditation and visualization. They tell me that:

No meditation is complete without visualization.
Anyone who meditates without visualization is getting
only 10 per cent of the benefits of meditation and
tapping only an infinitesimal fraction of the benefits.
And anyone who supplements their practice of feng
shui with visualizations of success symbols greatly
enhances the feng shui of their homes as well as of
their bodies and minds.

The mind has the power to create a physical reality that conforms to its thought patterns. And although spoken words and thoughts generate auspicious chi energy, images bring them into reality.

Mental visualization powerfully strengthens the practice of feng shui on both the surface and the inner levels of consciousness. This is predicated on the proposition that every physical reality on earth is a manifestation of energy, vibrating at different rates. The human mind controls this energy, so that, when properly harnessed, the human mind has the ability to create and shape physical reality through words and mental pictures.

The technique of visualization

Visualization is the technique of using your mind and your imagination to create pictures, images, ideas, of any desired object, outcome, symbol or scenario that makes you feel happy, auspicious and lucky. The deeper the placement of these images in your mind, the more powerful will be the imprint that is left on your mind. Expert visualization thus means being able to do this mental imaging at the deepest levels of consciousness.

Now, how these images are actually 'seen' in the mind differs from individual to individual. Different people do visualizations differently, so it is never necessary to worry unduly about whether you have got it right or not. As long as the images are real for you, that is all that matters.

Some people see the images as simply an idea, where the general mood of the scene comes through more strongly than any image, like a tableau. This kind of visualization is panoramic and often reveals a 'big picture person': someone who sees the whole picture. Such people are usually not worried about details – to them the overall outcome is more important. The panoramic person also tends to view their visualizations like a movie, one scene moving quickly to the next.

Another type of practitioner has to 'see' their visualizations according to images they have already seen. This group depends on the mind's memories of pictures or people they have encountered before: they take in all the details and their images seen in the mind tend to be colourful and rather vivid. These 'memories' can be of actual people and places or they may be based on pictures seen in movies and magazines or on the TV.

Some people see their images like a TV show. They create moving television screens inside their mind. Such people take a structured approach to visualization. The important thing to bear in mind is not to worry how you visualize. Do it according to what makes you comfortable. Use whatever props you feel are necessary, and often, these props come in very useful. Thus you can consider using coloured lights, pictures of beautiful objects and dream homes, and most importantly in feng shui, the auspicious symbols that work especially well in visualizations.

Visualization tends to be easier when you have a good idea of the kinds of images you wish to place inside your mind, and why. It is also a good idea to have a 'script' ready so you do not have to think very hard about what you want to visualize. If you already know what you wish to achieve from the visualization, and what symbols to think about, you will find your rate of success improving very fast.

Visualization is a way of moving into another level of consciousness. Planting pictures in the mind can only actualize outcomes if they are preceded by the mental relaxation which allows you to access your inner mind consciousness. Only then can the images reach the inner mind where chi energy is at its most potent. When you are in a state of relaxation and mental quiet, when nothing is distracting your mind, that is when you should use your imagination to visualize a clear image of something that you earnestly wish to have; or a situation you would like to see happen. One level of your mind will be saying that this is all illusion: your mind is not necessarily wrong, but illusions imprinted in the inner mind have the power to become real on the physical plane of reality.

The secret of successful visualization lies in the intensity of your belief and determination. This in turn affects the intensity of concentration and energy generated. The potential to manifest mental images into physical existence becomes as real as the energy created. Detailed images, firmly drawn, create strong positive energies. Sometimes it helps to think about the smells and sounds that are associated with a mental image in order to make it seem more real.

Using visualization

You can use visualization to bring almost anything you wish for into reality. It may be a possession, like a dream car or a new house. It may be a skill like dancing, or playing the piano, or speaking in public. It may be the desire to excel in an examination, to win a scholarship, to travel, to meet the right companion, or to cope with an emotional crisis.

You may be having trouble with your weight, or cannot cope with a faltering relationship, or you may be having severe problems at work. You may wish to give up smoking or some other habit you have identified as harmful ... anything at all can be quite effectively dealt with through the practice of meditative visualization. In these situations, the tremendous potential of visualization to change your life for the better is truly infinite.

Visualization harnesses the natural spiritual powers that exist within every human being. These powers work by activating basic human energy, or chi. It is possible to learn to mobilize and release these energies in a positive and controlled manner. In many people, these energies have already been activated, but they work in an unconscious manner so that one is not really aware of them. Nevertheless, they are powerful in their manifestations. Unfortunately the result of this unconscious use of creative visualization can be and usually is negative, and often even self-destructive. This is because all of us possess some pretty negative images in our minds. We are taught from a young age to set limits on our thinking. We expect the worst, fear the unknown, doubt ourselves, distrust our natural instincts. We can be stingy with our approval, and in the process can undermine our confidence and belittle our expectations – as a result of which, all the imagined outcomes we *see* in our minds tend to be *worst case scenarios*. So most visualizations are negative. Those who consciously or unconsciously practise this form of visualization deprive themselves of the vibrancy of happiness that comes with fulfilment, success, optimism, love, achievement and satisfaction.

Positive visualization done in a controlled manner can change all that. Visualization is a technique that can be mastered. Once you understand the fundamental power of picture images projected in the mind, and you practise it with optimism, cheerfulness and a happy disposition, you will literally have it in your power to create phenomenal occurrences in your life. Usually to an extent that will surprise and delight you.

The key to success in visualization is the ability

to focus your thoughts.

The picture in your mind must be sharp and clear. The goal or

situation as you want it to be must not be hazy and uncertain.

There must be intensity of belief, relaxed concentration and quiet

determination. The mental image must not be diluted by doubt or

ambivalence. Your attitude must be positive and confident.

And here is where the preliminary work you undertake in mentally reprogramming yourself into a more confident person through affirmations and other exercises is so useful. The meditative exercises which put you into comfortable contact with your inner wisdom adds to the success of your visualization efforts.

Visualization works best when you are deeply relaxed. The more relaxed you are, the purer will be the energy harnessed, and this greatly facilitates manifestation. The idea is to create pictures with a totally relaxed mind and body that is free of all tension and stress. Visualization then penetrates the deepest levels of the mind. This requires you to slow down your breathing, which in turn slows down your brain waves. This deeper level, as we saw earlier, is generally referred to as the *alpha level*. Your normal waking level is the beta level, but it is at the alpha level that visualization becomes truly powerful.

There are many different ways of reaching the alpha level. Those familiar with meditation or who practise yoga should know some of these methods. For those of you who wish to do so, the chapter on meditation should be of real help. From there you can devise your own methods of reaching the alpha level.

Find a secluded, undisturbed place and then get into a comfortable position, either sitting or lying down. Wear something loose and comfortable. Sometimes I play some soothing baroque music in the background. Then I gently close my eyes, tune into my breathing and gradually slow it down. I do this very slowly, taking my time, and I visualize my brain waves slowing down from about 14 cycles per minute to about three cycles per minute. I visualize the *wheel of life* turning in a clockwise direction as I slow down my breath and my brain waves. The sensation of heaviness overtakes me as I feel all my muscles, limbs and body relax. I stay in this state of mind, with a picture of the wheel of life turning slowly in my mind.

The sacred wheel of life is shown opposite. This is an auspicious sign, believed to be one of the eight images found on the footprints of Buddha. It is variously referred to as the Wheel of Life, the Wheel of Truth, the Wheel of a Thousand Spokes and the Wheel of the Cosmos. The wheel

symbolizes noble and wise truths. Some say it symbolizes the Buddha that lies inside every human being. The spokes of the wheel represent rays of sacred light emanating from our own Buddha nature and the turning of the wheel represents doctrines that explain the true nature of reality.

From our perspective the wheel represents the inner feng shui of the mind. The wheel signifies overcoming the three poisons of existence, which emanate from the ten directions – the eight directions of the compass, and also downwards and upwards. The three poisons of ignorance, anger and attachment, as we saw earlier, are considered to be the root causes of human suffering.

Visualization of this cosmic wheel symbol signifies attaining peace of mind and growing awareness of our own wisdom. It is particularly suitable for those who are hoping to experience insights and realizations that address the true meaning of reality.

It helps to breathe deeply and to follow your breath. Feel it as it moves in and out of your body. Imagine, as you breathe in, that a shining white light is flowing into your body, relaxing you from your toes to the tips of your fingers and washing you in a warm glow of well-being. When you breathe out, do so very slowly and imagine

that all tension, anger, worry and exhaustion are leaving
your body. Remember there is no rush when you breathe
in and out. Stay with this breathing exercise and keep the
image of the wheel, brightly lit up now, in your mind.

Make this a daily visualization exercise until it becomes comfortable.
Later you can picture the wheel sending out rays of light in the eight
directions of the compass along the spokes, and also downwards and
upwards. This energizes the cosmic chi from the ten directions. It is a very
auspicious meditative visualization.

Deep breathing and alpha level

Deep breathing is a beneficial adjunct to this visualization.

Imagine a balloon inside your tummy, so that as you
breathe in you feel the balloon expanding and getting
bigger; and as you breathe out feel it deflating. This
brings the breath deep into your abdominal chakra.
After a while you will drift into a rhythmic relaxation that
is very delightful.

Sometimes it helps to imagine yourself floating gently
in water, or feeling a gentle breeze caressing your cheeks
or falling like a leaf to the ground. Gently count down
from ten to one. Imagine the number in front of you, or
if it helps think of yourself going down on an escalator.
Tell yourself you are going down into your alpha level.

Feng shui visualizations can be on any subject. They can be at any level
of the human experience – physical, emotional, mental or spiritual. To
make the most out of visualization techniques you should establish your
motivations from the start. Get your goals sorted out clearly and succinctly.

What do you want this practice to achieve for you?

- Do you want to picture yourself getting a brand-new home?
- Do you wish for a more interesting new job with better prospects?
- Are you dreaming of gaining a place in a university of your choice?
- Do you desperately need a scholarship?
- Do you want romance and love in your life?
- Are your thoughts being consumed with the promotion you are after?
- Do you want to travel, have more money, win an important election?

In terms of aspirations, any kind of 'winning' scenario can be visualized into reality. So daydream as much as you want. Be imaginative. Fantasize. You can let your spirits soar with each new picture that comes into your mind. Let the pictures that you create excite and thrill you. Feel the joy and the pleasure of attaining your goals and desires. Pretend you already have whatever it is you are visualizing – make the pictures colourful and exciting. In short, let your imagination flow towards an outcome that will bring you fulfilment. You can also speak words to that effect if you feel they will strengthen your visualization outcomes.

If you find it difficult to create pictures in your mind, do not get too stressed about it. It is an art that requires practice. If you are doing it for the first time, do not be discouraged when you experience difficulty at first.

Don't try too hard, be relaxed.

Remember that not everyone does this imaging in exactly the same way. Some see clear, sharp photographs in their mind. Others imagine a mental TV programme with themselves as the star. For yet others, visualizing means getting impressions only - much like the Impressionist paintings of Monet or Pissarro. Some people think about a situation or scenery in a general sort of way. Try all the different methods. Something that suits you will emerge. Just do not get all tensed up.

Start with simple visualizations.

Working with colours

Colour in feng shui is vibration, and different colours have different vibrations. Since colours vibrate at different rates, each has its own signature frequency. Each colour also has its own wave pattern, and some are more clearly visible than others. For instance red is a brighter colour than yellow. Blue has a greater intensity than brown.

These colour 'vibes' are never good or bad in themselves. It is when colours interact with the vibrations of your inner essence and with the spirit of your thought forms that they exhibit compatibility or incompatibility. This interaction should be harmonious, just as the harmony of elements expresses itself in compatible or incompatible chi in the environment.

To harness the good feng shui of compatible and harmonious colours we should ensure that discordant notes do not intrude into the inner mind, especially during meditative visualization sessions.

Colour equivalents of the five elements

In feng shui colours have layers of meanings, the first of which has to do with the colour equivalents of the five elements. Thus red is associated with the element of fire, and blue signifies water. Green is wood while yellow is earth and white is metal. The in-between shades of these colours express the intensity of element symbolism. Red and white are also yang colours, while black and blue are yin colours.

One of the most effective ways of attracting different types of luck is to visualize rays of coloured light coming towards you.

Take a compass and get yourself oriented to the eight different directions, marking these directions around you if necessary. Then visualize receiving beautiful soft rays of colours coming towards you from the eight directions. Imagine yourself at the centre, with the directions surrounding you. Think of these rays of light entering your body via the top of your head and dissolving into your body through the crown chakra. These rays of light are

coloured according to the directions they come from.
Hence you can visualize

- red beams coming from the south and creating recognition luck;
- dark yellow beams coming from the south-west to bring you romance luck;
- light yellow beams coming from the north-east to bring you wisdom luck;
- leaf green beams coming from the south-east to attract wealth luck;
- dark green beams coming from the east to bring good descendants luck;
- white beams coming from the west and bringing pure health chi;
- white beams coming from the north-west bringing vital heaven luck.

Colour equivalents of planes of consciousness

Colours also reflect the different planes of consciousness and this arises from their different rates of vibration as well as the colours of the chakras of the human body. Chakras represent orbs of intense concentrations of chi.

At the root chakra, which is also the base level of consciousness, the colour is *red*. This is followed by *orange* at the lower abdominal level. At the next plane, which coincides with the solar plexus, the colour is a *golden yellow*. These are the three colours of the base chakras, and visualizing these colours while focusing attention on the lower part of the body is exceedingly beneficial for raising the chi of material enjoyment. Think of them as coloured orbs of bright light and as they radiate outwards, visualize yourself being filled with strong sense consciousness.

The upper chakras, which represent the higher planes of consciousness, begin at the heart chakra where the colour intensity is *green*. Immediately above this is the throat chakra where the colour intensity is a *light blue*. The next level is the second highest plane of consciousness and this is the place of the third or inner eye. The colour intensity here is *lilac*. Above this is the crown chakra, the highest level of consciousness; here the colour intensity is either *white or violet*. White is a very special colour because it encompasses the colours of all seven chakras, which correspond to the colours of the rainbow. So white signifies purity, spirituality and wholeness and at a deeper level implies that mastery of all planes of consciousness has been attained.

In addition you can visualize purple- (or violet-) to lilac-coloured beams coming from the sky above, bringing down rays of spiritual healing from the universe. These rays enter through the crown chakra into your mind and body, bathing you with an uplifting feeling of creativity. Lilac beams always possess high ethereal energy, which is very spiritual.

From the ground below you, visualize dark red or earth-coloured rays of light coming upwards and forming a halo of light around your base. This represents earth energy which ensures that you stay grounded in your visualization exercise. Staying grounded ensures that you are mentally alert throughout the exercise.

So now you know the meanings of the colours, how do you ensure their compatibility with your inner essence? Contrary to what you may think, this has nothing to do with your date of birth or astrological charts. Inner feng shui transcends the pull of gravity, and so dates and times of birth exert little influence on the compatibility of colours. Instead harmony is achieved according to your motivations, your moods and your levels of consciousness. For instance while you use white light to create an aura of purity and protection (and it is always safe to use white light meditation), you should start your meditations by tuning into a sphere of colour for any particular session. On certain days certain colours work better than on other days.

When you are feeling grey and depressed, which are very yin feelings, you might want to meditate on red light, which bathes you with strong earthy yang energy! And when you are feeling excessively loud and energetic you might want to meditate on cool greens of the heart or cool blues of the throat chakras. In any case finding your own personal favourite colour is something you have to work at on your own. Spend some time discovering the colour or colours that work best for you.

So now we can start.

Gently close your eyes. Relax. Breathe deeply. Think of your favourite colour. It can be any colour. Then imagine yourself surrounded, embraced and bathed in this colour. If it is blue, think of a beautiful blue light that wraps itself around you. Think of the blue sky. Hold the vision as long as possible. At first just doing this will seem difficult, but you will get better at it. If other thoughts wander in, gently push those thoughts and distracting pictures away, and focus again on the beautiful blue light that surrounds you. It helps to look at a blue light before trying to visualize it in your mind. When you have succeeded with one colour, move on to others ... red ... green ... yellow ... orange ... lilac ... and purple, the colours of the rainbow, before coming back to the white light. Experiment with all colours.

Each colour has its own attributes and none of the colours will hurt you in visualization. But you have to experiment with them until you discover the one that is most compatible with your inner essence. If you find this difficult, go back to white light. Some people can work with many different colours while others can work only with the white light. This is because white light symbolizes the ultimate yang energy of the Chien trigram, the premier trigram of the *I Ching*, which implies help, luck and blessings from heaven.

Successfully visualizing the white light and holding it in your mind is always beneficial. You will find it very easy to go from visualizing white light to visualizing other images. So you can begin all your visualization exercises with an image of yourself surrounded by bright white light. Think of it as a protective cocoon, which envelops you in a warm glow of tranquillity. Feel the white light protecting and embracing you, filling your whole being with pure and harmonious thoughts. One of the side effects of white light meditation is the welling up of a great compassion and kindness for all living beings. When you feel this sentiment rising within you it is the surest indication that spiritual awareness has begun.

A private sanctuary

The next visualization to work on is the creation of a very private place which you can think of as your sanctuary. Use your mind to create this tranquil mental paradise, a place of your own invention, a place you can think of and retreat to each time you wish to relax or where you can have a few moments to clarify your thoughts, motivations in life and your aspirations. People have their own ideas about their private utopia, their personal Shangri-La. Some people love the sea, others dream of a place hidden in the mountains. Yet others dream of a magic garden filled to overflowing with flowers and fruit trees... Sometimes the imagination runs riot and we dream of a land far away in outer space, where hi tech gadgets abound and where luxury and peace take on totally strange new dimensions...

This private sanctuary is your own creation so you can make it any kind of place you like. Good feng shui can be created in any kind of space. Places need not be pristine and neat and uncluttered to have good feng shui. The qualities of chi, real or emanating from the mind, are founded on balance, harmony and thought vibrations. Physical objects do give off vibrations but these vary according to the level of yin and yang they possess as well as their intrinsic elemental energy. Thus neat places can have bad feng shui just as cluttered places can enjoy excellent feng shui.

So when you think of your private sanctuary, create something in your mind that makes you feel comfortable, warm and safe. Here are some suggestions ...

- a beautiful tropical beach with the waves gently lapping is a restful shade of blue and white;

- a cool mountain resort where the air is clean and fresh and the green of the trees is especially soothing;
- rolling countryside in the spring where carpets of daffodils stretch as far as the eye can see;
- an idyllic river scene where you can relax on soft green grass beside a clear gurgling brook;
- a large mansion with a big spacious room;
- a small cottage in the country with a friendly kitchen.

Any scene that you personally associate with pleasant sensations and feelings can be the basis of your private sanctuary. So pull a scene into your consciousness and focus in on it.

Once again it is helpful to become very relaxed. Use pictures of beautiful scenery to help you create inspiring paradise locations. My private sanctuary is a mountain scene. I have always loved the mountains, especially snow-capped mountains. When I discovered this affinity, it really surprised me because I was born and bred in a tropical country where the climate is hot and humid – a far cry from the feel of snowy mountains. For years I indulged my love of mountains by going on winter ski holidays which always made me feel happy. So for me, my private sanctuary is a cave deep in the white mountains of the Himalayas.

I have mentally travelled to this sanctuary many thousands of times. Over the years this cave has been where I go to recharge my batteries and energize myself. Although it has been in my consciousness for as long as I can remember, it is not based on any picture or scene I have ever seen. The snow-covered peaks lie in the distance, and all round me are high mountains. Below are fields of green that seem to have been terraced for cultivation … I picture myself sitting on a ledge just outside the cave drinking in the magic of the mountains. In front of me is an image of a frail old man sitting in meditation. I used to think of him as my inner guide, a spiritual emanation of some kind, and I've always known that he is someone I love beyond space and time. So that cave is my safe and very private sanctuary.

Allow your mind free flow in this exercise. You will find that there is always some kind of scene that you have an uncanny affinity with. Do not force yourself to latch on to anything just so that you can have a place. Take your time, and practise with the scene in your mind until you are able to come to your private sanctuary merely by thinking it ... and then sitting there you can begin to undertake your visualizations.

Setting goals before you start

Be very clear what you are visualizing to achieve. This is not a practice to be taken lightly. In the beginning, keep your goals simple. People I know who have used the technique successfully started with very modest aspirations. So you may wish to cope with the daily stress of working life, like feelings of irritation, anger, annoyance and frustration. For dealing with this sort of stress, think of yourself as being totally relaxed and being able to cope with temper tantrums and petty trivialities. If the problem is a recalcitrant child, you can picture yourself being very patient. If it is an unreasonable husband or wife, think of rising above the situation, and when the problem is a difficult or hostile situation involving another person, visualize yourself surrounded by goodwill and love. In every instance, the act of relaxing and mentally picturing a happy outcome while you are in your sanctuary will diffuse the problem in your mind. This quickly leads to a calming effect on your physical reality.

Keeping goals easy at first also empowers you with fantastic motivating energy. This is because you will not have to cope with negative resistance within yourself. Deep-rooted doubts are bound to surface. A certain amount of scepticism; a carryover of negative conditioning; or more likely, merely ignorance of the mind's vast powers and a natural inclination to disbelief. While such feelings are understandable, it requires time to overcome them and they tend to slow down the effectiveness of the process.

Keeping initial goals easy will reinforce your belief in the technique and your belief in your power to transform your visions into reality. Later, as you gain more confidence in yourself, your inner conscious belief in your own power will grow. Then you can start to take on more difficult problems or be more ambitious in your wants and your dreams.

Think things through before you start. It is important that what you visualize is truly, genuinely what you want. Clarify your thoughts thoroughly. Be very sure!

It is not necessary to worry about *how* goals can be attained, or how what you wish for can materialize. Do not weaken your visualizations with doubts caused by the rational thinking mind. Just be very clear about the end result you wish for and concentrate on that. Let the chi you are releasing into the vast universe through your visualization work out the ways and means for you.

> Decide on something you would like to have, something you wish to work towards achieving: an ambition you wish to realize, a relationship you wish to improve ... at any level and in whatever aspect of your life. It can be a job; a dream house or car; increased prosperity; a happier state of mind; a cure for a disease; a slimmer body; a new relationship; better communication with those you love; nicer children ... anything at all.

Remember that the process involves creating positive chi. Confidence in its outcome, a genuine belief, a firm determination and a relaxed, detached attitude towards its positive result are vital ingredients of success. It is important not to be tense or desperate about aspirations as well as wanting what you visualize. Half-hearted visualizations lack energy and focus and are unlikely to succeed. To generate vibrations for success, you must imbue your visualizations with plenty of positive encouragement and affirmations.

- Believe that what you desire is very real and is absolutely possible.

- Believe that you truly deserve and truthfully want what you ask for.

Continue with your efforts until you achieve the goal. Sometimes you will find fulfilment almost immediately. Sometimes it takes longer. Sometimes your goals may change or you lose interest halfway. If and when this happens, do not feel bad. Just acknowledge it and move on. Changing your mind is perfectly acceptable. You can change your goals as often as you wish. Just set new goals and begin again.

Clever goal setting

Successful feng shui visualization depends on how well you establish your goals. It is not always easy to know what you really want. What you wish for can also change at different stages of your life. Be patient with yourself when trying to sort out what is and is not important to you. Take your time to think through your priorities. It is understandable that aspirations and ambitions change with time and circumstance. The human psyche is fickle and frivolous, especially when we are young and want many different things. We are greedy for life and for all its glittering products, status symbols and rich lifestyles.

Do not feel there is anything wrong with wanting to keep up with the Joneses. It is natural to desire what you see others enjoying. But you must be honest with yourself. Don't operate at two levels of wishes. Don't say you don't need to be rich when you desperately want to be just that! I have always been surprised when people say to me, 'Ah but I am sure you don't write for the money?' and I look at them perplexed, before saying, 'Oh yes I do, but I also write to fulfil my own mission ... but yes, money is part of what I want to achieve.' I point this out because I must have come across literally thousands of people who say to me they don't want money, that it's not the money that counts, and statements like that. I often want to say if you don't want money then why are you asking me to activate your feng shui wealth corners and why are you complaining about your lack of income?

When there is this inherent dishonesty, it is difficult for your aspirations to become actualized. Feng shui chi works the same way. Unless you acknowledge that you want something and believe you deserve to get it, and you don't feel guilty or bad about wanting it, only then will you obtain what you want. But it is not necessary to measure your wants only in terms of what others have. Look on material possessions as the tangible manifestation of what motivates us to work, to strive, and to aim for success.

In today's world, it is not surprising that most of us have a profusion of needs and aspirations. There are many choices facing us. We are constantly subjected to a barrage of tantalizing possibilities through advertising and media promotions. Truly the modern era is full of temptations. Is it any wonder that we wish to reach out and possess some of the goodies available? Fortunately both feng shui and visualization work best when our wants and desires are strong and clear, and are accompanied by the conviction that what we want is attainable. At the same time we must not be addicted to our wants. While giving them weight, we cannot invest too much emotional energy in them.

Writing down your aspirations

Goal setting therefore requires clear-mindedness. Some planning is called for. I have found that the best way to start is to write down all that you want from life in an organized way. Keep goals simple and straightforward. One way is to categorize them under meaningful headings, listed in a ranking of personal importance:

> Money. Career. Lifestyle. Relationships. Leisure. Family. Personal growth. Love. Power. Possessions. Recognition. Specific achievements. Winning. Health. Children. Marriage.

Study the list carefully and think through it. Expand on the areas of your life that seem important to you and try to be specific. Differentiate between long-term and short-term goals. And be honest with yourself. Do not feel you have to like what others like, want what others want. You could be setting yourself up for disappointment.

Try to sort out in your mind what exactly will make *you* happy. Goal setting on paper requires soul searching and serious thought. If you can actually sit down and plan all you want to achieve during various time frames and stages of your life, you will imbue the process with real energy. The act of sitting down and putting pen to paper activates the inner motivations of your mind, so that a deeper wisdom starts to guide you. When listing your goals, explore your inner mind thoroughly. Do not ignore the small voice coming from inside your head, which attempts to speak to you. Do not ignore your instinct. Don't let confusion get in the way either.

Stay with the process of goal setting. As you work through the headings on your list, you will soon get the knack of it. Your thoughts will become focused. You will empower your mind by giving it a sense of real purpose.

Making it work for you

There are no secrets to making visualization work for you. Regular practice, a relaxed approach and a belief in the fundamental empowerment of the mind through usage are all that you need for eventual success.

Make it an integral part of your daily routine. Do it at least once a day either in the mornings just before getting out of bed, or in the late evenings just before falling asleep. These are the moments when you will be the most relaxed and when your attitude is most conducive to embarking on a journey into your mind.

Always start by being extremely relaxed and positive.
Allow your mind to wander a little, all the time being
aware of the thoughts that seemingly come from
nowhere. This is part of your inner knowledge seeking to
surface from within your subconscious. Although the
mind is wandering, follow your thoughts so you will be

making pathways into the inner mind. You never know what might surface when you least expect it.

Visualization works best when you are being guided by your inner wisdom. Long-dormant powers will slowly creep into your conscious mind. So always trust your impulses. If you feel uncomfortable, take time to relax and breathe deeply. If you feel overcome by an inexplicable sense of well-being, accept this feeling also.

If you have difficulty relaxing, use the breathing method to develop focused concentration. Establish a rhythm of breathing. Suggest that your brain waves slow down by picturing a series of steep Ws stretching into shallower Ws. This is an effective visualization for accessing your alpha levels. Or count backwards from ten to one, relaxing further at each number. You will soon find yourself ready actively to create pictures in your mind. Spend as long as you like at this stage. Do not rush. If other images intrude either accept them or gently push them away. Do not ever feel discouraged. Be patient and consciously encourage yourself with positive statements.

Developing a daily habit

Make visualization a daily habit. Do it until it becomes part of your everyday routine – like brushing your hair, or washing your hands before you eat. Aim at achieving a positive outlook to help you achieve specific goals. Practise visualization without getting addicted to it. Do not lose your sense of harmony and balance. Believe in its effectiveness but do not get too intense about it. And never lose your sense of humour.

Constantly reaffirm your positive view of the universe. Say your favourite affirmations to yourself throughout the day, silently or aloud – when getting dressed, when driving to work, sitting at your desk, at a dinner party. Before long you will have built a strongly positive inner conscious mind that will make you very receptive to all the good fortune you wish for.

Use modern technology to assist you. Record your favourite words and sentences on tape then play them back just before retiring each night. Or write positive affirmations in your diary. Practise saying positive things with friends and colleagues. Make yourself aware of other people's good qualities and attributes. Get used to saying uplifting, encouraging things to others.

Be sure you are sincere in the compliments you hand out. If at first you feel awkward about this outflowing of love, stay with it. It takes a bit of getting used to, but it is one of the most powerful ways of creating positive vibrations and energies. Try to make strong positive statements a standard feature of your conversation patterns. I promise you will be amazed at the dramatic changes in the quality of your relationships. You will become a lighter, happier person.

It is not necessary to rush. And if you sense yourself feeling strongly negative sometimes, do not force yourself. A lifetime's conditioning as far as behaviour and response patterns are concerned cannot be overturned suddenly. Be patient. Also, don't try to be positive when you are feeling angry or upset. Allow these feelings to come out. If you don't let them out, they do not go away. They merely get more deeply embedded inside you – and this sort of unhealthy bottling up is so harmful. It is never easy convincing yourself that that person who knifed you in the back deserves your goodwill when what you really want to do is happily strangle him. It is not easy ... but try sending generous doses of goodwill towards your so-called enemies. It really is the best way of neutralizing the negative vibrations generated by enmity.

Do not adopt a martyr complex either. When you feel anger and frustration, you have every right to let off steam. But having got it out of your system, wait for your mood to mellow, then reaffirm soothing, calming statements to yourself. You should always regain your balance, so the human chi flows within you can move smoothly. Habitual calming of your anger and frustrations does much to protect the health and balance of your inner mind. And because your inner mind is so precious to your general well-being, it deserves special and loving care.

Going with the flow

Take a relaxed attitude towards your goals, no matter how crucial they may seem to you at any moment in time: be willing to redefine them if and when something better comes along. Going with the flow means being flexible in your outlook and keeping your horizons tuned to the environment so that if necessary you can change direction.

If you have a lot of emotional baggage riding on whether you attain your goal, you will tend to work against yourself. Inherent in your fear of failure will be the inadvertent creation of negative energy. You may actually be energizing the idea of *not* getting what you so badly want. Better then to be relaxed and gently confident. Better to go with the flow. Remember that the river of life often takes a winding course. Sometimes it may even appear to be flowing in the wrong direction. Yet if you go with the flow, it is an easier and more harmonious ride than trying to struggle against the currents. You will reach your destination in the end.

If you are finding it hard to let go, it may be useful to examine your feelings of fear more closely. Ask yourself what exactly you fear about not achieving your goals. Work on your fears using conscious relaxation and carefully worded affirmative statements that increase your confidence and heighten your sense of security.

All this does not mean you do not have a strong desire for what you creatively visualize. What is important is that the desire must not be obsessive. If you feel a sense of desperation that creates conflicting emotions, you must first resolve this conflict. Examine your attitudes closely. If you perceive an *urgent* need to get what you want, *back off a little*. Make an effort to be a little more detached. Maybe your inner wisdom is trying to tell you something. Perhaps there is another way, another goal that will be better for you in the long run. Maybe it is something you may not even have considered.

Mental spring-cleaning

Over the years, we accumulate mental excess baggage which creates hindrances in the mind. These blocks constrict the natural flow and rhythm of thought patterns and hamper the attainment of objectives.

Mental blockages are caused by repressed emotions, like fear, guilt, resentment, anger and frustration arising from disappointments, the loss of a dear one, perceived injustices ... and from constant negative programming. There is a lifetime of negative programming behind all of us. We believe the world is not a safe place. We believe life has to be a struggle. We believe we have to suffer, that it is noble to be poor, that having fun is wrong, that love is dangerous because we will get hurt ... that politics is dirty, that money is the root of all evil, that life is fated.

These are beliefs. Nothing more. They are not objective truths. They are true only if you believe they are true. Mental blockages such as these are usually deep-rooted. They are emotional hindrances that subdue our inherent spirit and suppress our natural vitality. They really are bad news. Get rid of them! Don't allow beliefs such as these to damage your self-esteem and self-worth.

Besides, they make us scared to dream and to hope. Often the fear of failure and of being ridiculed is so strong that it can even cause illnesses. All of these things I describe are manifestations of a fragile and deluded ego, that is all.

To get the current of energy flowing again, we must simply get rid of these beliefs. I call it the spring-cleaning of the mind. The first step is to accept our personal limiting attitudes and beliefs.

Identify the true nature of your fears. Usually, focusing on the constrictive beliefs and acknowledging the feelings that surround them are sufficient to make the negative attitude slowly dissolve and disappear. This is the clearing process, and it works wonderful magic in freeing us from the severely inhibiting barriers that hamper achievement. Mental spring-cleaning is uplifting as it transforms your world view as well as your view of yourself. It brings all that you have ever secretly wanted suddenly, miraculously within reach.

Removing other barriers

There are other kinds of emotional baggage – like grudges caused by repressed anger and resentments – that also need to be cleared. This is like throwing garbage out of your home instead of allowing it to accumulate into a huge pile of killing energy. Usually, carrying a grudge and allowing hostile thoughts to fester soaks up all the precious good energy inside you. It is exhausting maintaining negative feelings towards those we believe have harmed us, mistreated us, done us an injustice or badmouthed us. There is every justification to feel aggrieved. Ours is a righteous ire. It feels good, even, to be angry. But if you think it through, it really does feel better to create release by letting go, by forgetting and forgiving. This allows bad energy to dissipate, making way for good energy.

Forgiveness creates a powerful sense of liberation because it is like breaking down a dam. Many people find it quite miraculous to free themselves of the burdens of accumulated resentment and hostility. Some have described the experience as not unlike the dropping of heavy baggage off their backs.

This is particularly relevant when your visualizations involve other people in your scenario of success, e.g. when the achievement of your goals requires the approval, blessing, consent or help of people who you might feel are against you. Unless you first undertake clearing exercises to diffuse negative energies surrounding the feeling, your success could get blocked!

Try sending symbols of love and goodwill towards these people. Picture a host of white doves, hearts, even kisses flowing through the cosmos towards those you feel are not well disposed towards you. Soften your attitude when you use this visualization. Let go completely of feelings of fear and anger. Replace them with goodwill.

Visualizing for abundance

This particular visualization assumes the universe is totally plentiful and abundant. It assumes that you and I and everyone else on this earth were born with an entitlement to share in this abundance. Everything we need and want can become part of our physical reality. If you believe this, it will be so. If you really desire what you ask for, you will get it.

It is important to believe you deserve abundance in all its manifestations. It is like prosperity programming, which can work only if you shed off all vestiges of the poverty programming that many of us carry around as unwanted baggage. The belief that life is full of suffering, that we cannot have everything we want, that we should not be too greedy when the rest of the world is starving, that we should feel guilty about wanting the luxuries of life ... these are foolish attitudes and serve only to perpetuate the scarcity thinking that is so widespread.

The truth is that the earth is simply overflowing with abundance and nourishing prosperity. This is the natural state of things. Prosperity thinking invokes the positive energies of the earth and creates the aura of abundance. Taking this attitude reinforces the visualization of a plentiful universe. This conviction has the power to manifest great riches into our lives, but it requires a transformation of belief systems. You have to convince your inner space consciousness that ours is truly an abundant universe and that you want to participate in this abundance.

I am also a great believer in the self-fulfilling prophecy. I have discovered that if I believe something strongly enough, be it good or bad, something will surely happen. I shrug off anything negative as so much nonsense. Whether they are predictions or opinions, I never allow them to gather any energy in my mind by thinking of them. I simply trash them. Delete them from my mind.

At first, this may seem far-fetched and unrealistic. Practising psychologists disapprove of this sort of attitude: they object to people building walls around themselves, creating mental blocks. I have thought this through a great deal and have come to the conclusion that if it makes me a happier, more optimistic person, why shouldn't I create protective psychic shields around myself? Why should I be pessimistic when I am better off being optimistic? In any case, the mind co-operates. If you tell it to ignore foolish prophecies, disbelieve predictions of negative outcomes, and forget bad memories of failures and disappointments, the mind accepts your attitude, and will even help you along.

Each time I need to undertake a project or indulge myself, I somehow succeed in finding the money to do it. Instead of worrying about how I can possibly finance my ambitions, I focus instead on all the things I have to work at to achieve them. And, when I am ready for it, the money always comes: sometimes in a roundabout way – but still it comes. When I needed money to go to Harvard, I got a UN fellowship three days before I left. When I needed financing to buy my Dragon Seed department store, I found the money somehow. When I needed an international publisher for my books the moment I was ready for it, a publisher materialized in my life. In all these instances I never once doubted that a happy outcome would happen...

As for all your memories, be equally selective in the things you wax nostalgic about. Remember the Barbra Streisand song about memories? Simply choose to forget all those events that caused you pain and reinforced your insecurities. With this strong attitude in place you are now ready to try out the different visualizations in the workshops of the next chapter.

Part III

7.

Workshops for inner feng shui practice

Close your eyes and walk into your secret world

The fantasy valley of your inner mind

A quiet place for gentle dreaming

A magic mirror through which you watch yourself

Transform into the beautiful person

You were always meant to be

Rich in consciousness awareness, full of love,

Laughter, and a sense of total abundance

The preliminaries

I have designed a series of guided sessions to help you get started on your feng shui visualization programme. Read through all the exercises and then tape them on a cassette. Play some soothing music in the background. I have discovered that baroque music is particularly effective for facilitating inner space consciousness. Or if you wish you can listen to the mandala music of the Colorado-based Japanese synthesist Kitaro. Music played on any stringed instrument can also be used.

In the beginning, please do these visualizations in the correct order. Find a suitable place in your home or use the special room set aside for your meditation practice. The room must be relatively quiet; try to arrange not to be disturbed. If you wish, have a bath or shower before you start, then wear comfortable clean clothes. These special visualization sessions are best done in the late evenings or very early mornings.

Purifying the space before you start

To enhance the feeling of peace and harmonious well-being in your meditation space, it is a good idea to purify the place before you start. If you are using the room for the first time, cleanse the space of all negative energies by using a singing bowl or bell which is made from seven types of metal (including gold and silver).

Walk round the periphery of the room three times in a clockwise direction striking the bowl and allowing the sounds to absorb any bad energy that has accumulated in the room.

If you do not have a suitable singing bell or bowl, use a mixture of salt and rice grains and throw these at the base of the walls of the room. This need only be done the first time you use the room for meditation. This ritual appeases wandering spirits and ensures they will not disturb your mind when you meditate.

To purify the room and make the atmosphere soft and conducive, you can do any of the following:

- Spray lavender mist into the room, or burn lavender oil. Lavender is very soothing and it enhances the receptivity of inner mind consciousness. If you know of other oils that are especially good for you, please select the oils of your choice.

- Burn pure incense made from herbs taken from the mountains. My favourite is Himalayan mountaintop incense, which comes from the Solu Khumbu region. This is said to be the holiest part of the mountain and it lies about 14,000 feet above sea level. The scent of this incense is amazingly pure and magical.
- Burn sandalwood incense. This was the original incense used by the Chinese to purify their space, and if you can find sandalwood powder it is a good idea to use it occasionally even if you do not like the smell.

Before I start, I always purify the space with my singing bowl and Himalayan incense. Mine comes from the Lawado region, which is part of Solu Khumbu. This cave and this region have special meaning for me.

Prepare your meditation cushion as described on p. 117.

Establishing your orientation

For optimum results from your meditation and visualization exercises, you should establish your orientation according to feng shui. Thus the meditation cushion should be placed in such a way that when you sit on it and gaze forward, your head is facing in a direction that is deemed to be the most conducive for you based on the Kua or 8 Mansions formula. This means that chi coming towards you will be the most auspicious. Use the Kua number to find out your best visualization direction. The Kua number is worked out on the basis of your date of birth and gender.

The formula

Using 4 February as the date of the New Year for each year, take the last two digits of your year of birth, and add them, and keep adding the digits until you get a single digit.

If you are a male, deduct this number from 10 and the result is your Kua number.

If you are female add 5 and the result is your Kua number.

Example: 4 January 1963. Here the year of birth is actually 1964 because the date of birth shows that it was before 4 February, the Chinese New Year day (please note that I am using the Chinese solar calendar to get the cut-off date instead of the Chinese lunar year; this is because the solar calendar can also be used to work out the Kua number). So adding the last two digits of 1964 means 6 + 4 = 10 and 1 + 0 = 1.

For males, deduct from 10: 10 − 1 = 9 so the Kua number is 9.

For females, add 5: 5 + 1 = 6 so the Kua is 6.

For those born in year 2000 and beyond

The same formula is used except that for males you deduct the sum of the digits from 9 and for females you add 6 to the sum of the digits.

Example: 12 October 2000. Here the year of birth is 2000 and the last two digits add up to zero. So the Kua for males is 9 − 0 = 9 and for females it is 6 + 0 = 6.

Use the table here to find your most ideal meditation and visualization direction. For those with Kua number 5, the direction for males will be south-west and for females north-east.

Kua	1	2	3	4	5	6	7	8	9
Sit facing	north	south-west	south-east	east	s-w (women) n-e (men)	north-west	west	north-east	south

Getting started

Gently lower your eyes until they are nearly closed but not quite.

Look in front of you without straining. Place your gaze about a foot in front of you. Try not to close your eyes completely, as this tends to send you to sleep.

Breathe normally, watching your breath, and slowly breathe more deeply. Feel the slow rhythm of your breath, and then as you breathe in make a count of six: feel the air slowly filling your tummy. It is like a balloon inside your tummy. Feel it expand as it fills with your breath. Hold to a count of three and then gently breathe out to a count of six again, releasing the air with a sigh.

Do it again. Breathe in slowly to a count of six. Hold to a count of three. And breathe out slowly to a count of six. All the while you are getting more relaxed. As you breathe in, you feel yourself filling with pure new energy. As you breathe out, you feel yourself expelling all the tensions, stress, exhaustion and negative feelings of the day. Do it once more.

Now breathe in again to a count of six. You know that six is the number of the chien trigram and that it represents the greatest yang and the highest heaven. The energy associated with the number six is extremely auspicious. As you hold your breath, think of the auspiciousness of six and invoke its luck into your consciousness. And then breathe out with a long, gentle sigh.

You are starting to feel good now. Any tiredness is leaving you and you are beginning to resonate in consonance with the rhythm of your breath.

Figure of eight

Think of the figure eight superimposed upright on your body, and as you breathe in imagine the breath circling the top half of the eight; and as you breathe out, visualize the breath circling the bottom half of the eight. The centre of this figure of eight is where your solar plexus chakra is located. Do this gently and feel the rhythm and balance of the breath. The figure eight symbolizes the prosperity that will begin in the year 2004. Eight is also symbolically an excellent number for visualization since it represents a perfect balance between the material enjoyments of the physical world and the transcendental bliss of the spiritual world. This is therefore an excellent preliminary visualization.

Keep breathing until you are comfortable with this rhythm. Be consciously aware of the breath as it moves in along the path mapped out by the figure of eight and out of your body. Never force or in any way exert yourself. Don't try to hold your breath. Let the breathing be a natural process of your life force.

After a while, sense the feeling of calm and serenity which begins to wash over you. As you get more relaxed and comfortable, start to 'see' with your inner eye.

The first thing you see is a shining bright white light.

The light is just in front of you. The image is not unlike that of a spotlight shining directly above you. It creates a halo around your body, an invisible force field. This protects you, allowing nothing to disturb you as you make your journeys into your inner world.

The shining white light

Always begin with this visualization since it creates an invisible protective shield around your body and ensures that nothing from 'other realms' of existence comes to disturb you.

At this stage you can move on to other visualization exercises or if you like you can use the white light meditation to re-energize yourself. If this is what you wish to do then think of the white light moving through your body.

Picture the light at your toes, permeating every pore, every cell, energizing these cells as it lights them up. Feel the light energize your feet, then move slowly up your legs, up your thighs and into your pelvic area. Some people feel ticklish when they do this visualization, but everyone will feel recharged and reinvigorated as the light moves slowly up the lower body.

The energy of the white light is warm. It washes upward over all your organs, through your blood cells and capillaries. It moves up your chest and permeates your whole back. You feel it move down your hands and into your fingers. Then it moves up your neck and you know you are feeling very good and relaxed.

The white light then moves up to your face, lighting it so magnificently you feel luminous and strongly energized. You know you are very radiant now, and all tension, all stress, all anger and all negativity flow out of you. There is a feeling of lightness, kindness and happiness. Suddenly you really understand the incredible lightness of 'being'. So you stay with this feeling for a while and open your mind to whatever comes...

This is a very powerful visualization, which will engage and activate the natural chi inside you.

When you come out of the visualization allow some moments to rest before getting up.

Your perfect home – a private heaven

When you feel you are ready, use the preliminary visualization to get relaxed and receptive to further exercises. One excellent visualization is to create a perfect home for yourself, a private heaven.

First picture the white light in front of you. Focus on it for a few seconds and as you gaze at it imagine it dissolving into a picture of your very own private place. The scene which materializes in front of you will take shape spontaneously. It can be a Garden of Eden. Or it can be a fertile valley. Or it can be in the high mountains.

Everyone has their own idea of what represents their own pure environment. Occasionally I take myself up to 'heaven'. I picture myself flying up to the pure lands of the Buddhas which lie beyond the clouds... All of this occurs in my imagination but for me these scenes of 'heaven' are very real. I have perfect homes in the mountains and in the heavens as well. So let your own imagination lead you to your personal heaven. Here is one example:

Allow your mind to create the scene. When it emerges from the depth of your consciousness you will immediately recognize it. This beautiful, peaceful place is yours. This is *your* inner sanctuary, your paradise. And in this imaginary place you will build your private abode, a home where the feng shui is perfect. It is a place where chi enters from the most favourable directions, and where auspicious chi accumulates in abundance wherever you sleep, sit or eat. It is a place where water features and water flows are in perfect alignment with the home. Behind the house are high mountains and in front there is a beautiful flat garden at the edge of which a small stream with clean sparkling water flows past as if embracing the garden. Think of the stream of water as the green 'jade belt' which brings you auspicious good fortune.

The flat expanse of green grass is the bright hall, a special place which attracts the most auspicious energies of the universe. Here lucky chi gathers, becoming a major source of energy from where excellent sheng chi makes its way lazily into your home.

In the distance in front of the home are more hills, but they slope down towards the plain. On both sides of the home are hills, with those on the left being slightly higher than those on the right. It seems that your beautiful home is embraced by the loving presence of the celestial animals.

Behind, the celestial tortoise protects you with its powerful back shell which resembles a domed hill. To your left is the celestial green dragon, or *cheng lung*, which symbolizes all that is special about the earth's energy. To the right and in copulation with the dragon is the celestial white tiger and in front resembling a little footstool is the celestial crimson phoenix, which attracts opportunities into your life. These four creatures combine to create the most perfect orientation and arrangement of landscape for your perfect home in your perfect heaven.

Each day when you meditate on your perfect home you can add more features. Make this 'home' in your mind both comfortable and beautiful. Visualize it as furnished with every good fortune symbol. Give it as many rooms as you wish, with each room designed to satisfy some special need you have. For instance, you may have a music room, a games room, a swimming room, a gym and so forth. There can be as many bedrooms as you wish. When you visualize it, make your home as large and as spacious as you can imagine. There should be no limits to what you visualize. This is the best way to encourage your creativity to surface.

The hall of eight aspirations

Create a special room in your perfect home. Make it a perfect square and make it very beautiful. Picture this room as spacious, well lighted and peaceful. There is an entrance door and windows that look out to beautiful gardens, hills and rivers. The room has a marble floor and on the floor is a compass design made of mosaic tiles. It occupies the entire hall and all the eight directions are clearly marked out. From the markings on the floor it is easy for you to identify each of the eight directions

Think of each sector as one small grid. Visualize the floor as nine squares, with one square in the centre and three on each side of the wall. Altogether there are nine squares: this is known as a Lo Shu grid. The grid makes it easy for you to visualize this room as the Hall of Eight Aspirations. Each of the squares surrounding the centre square represents

LO SHU Grid

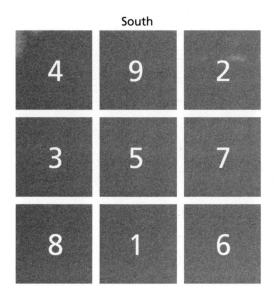

South

a compass direction as well as one major life aspiration.

Look at the Lo Shu grid shown here. Imagine this superimposed on the floor of your Hall of Eight Aspirations. Where the number 9 is on the floor, that is the south. This south square symbolizes the element of fire and the aspiration of being recognized and acknowledged. Starting with the south of the hall, move your attention slowly from one square to the next. Picture the square and then picture the actual hall itself. Move around the hall in a clockwise direction, following the guided visualization below.

So ... think of the number 9.

This is the south square. In your mind it corresponds to where the compass needle points south. Say to yourself very strongly that you are standing in the south corner of the Hall of Eight Aspirations. Then picture the wall in this square as bright red in colour. There is a very beautiful light here which stays perpetually turned on. This corner of the Hall of Eight Aspirations symbolizes widespread and favourable recognition of your talents and your capabilities. Imagine the light here shining brightly and imagine it growing in intensity each time you need the kind of luck which leads to recognition of your talents. If you wish to advance further then generate a picture of the trigram Li, which is the trigram of fire. This trigram has two solid lines embracing a broken line in the centre. Feel this strongly. Do this visualization when you are in line for promotion, when you are being interviewed for a job or when you require strong positive publicity for your work. Actresses, singers and just about anyone engaged in business or work that requires favourable publicity and fame will benefit from this visualization.

Next, think of the number 2.

This is the square that is next to 9 moving in a clockwise direction. The direction is south-west, and it is one of the most important corners in this hall because it symbolizes good fortune in all your relationships. This corner also represents love, romance and marriage luck. The element here is earth, which is produced by fire. Let the wall here be red as well or of an earth colour. In this corner visualize a large crystal globe so big it pulsates with energy. Imagine bright light emanating from the crystal activating the luck of this corner and filling the room with stunning good energy. This is also the corner represented by the powerful trigram Kun which signifies the zeal and spirit of the matriarch. Visualize it – three broken yin lines. Feel the power of this trigram very strongly pervading this corner. Your visualization will create extremely potent matriarchal chi which brings excellent relationships luck.

Next, move on to the number 7.

This symbolizes the west of the hall. This corner represents the luck of the next generation. Here the element is metal and the colour, which brings luck, is white or any other metallic colour. The trigram of this sector of the hall is Tui, made up of one broken yin line above two solid unbroken yang lines. Picture this trigram strongly, for it signifies joyousness. It stands for laughter, for rejoicing and celebration. It implies success and continuity of family through descendants, and its good name. More than anything Tui means gold, but not ordinary gold. The reference is symbolic, for gold here means virtuous offspring who bring fame, honour and happiness to the family. Good children are regarded as more precious than gold. When Tui gets energized there is harmony in the household. Siblings enjoy good relationships and children respect their elders. Husbands and wives get along and the mood of the home becomes serene and calm.

Activate Tui in your mentally created Hall of Eight Aspirations, strengthen it with a dose of chi by placing windchimes, bells or other metallic objects in this corner, and watch all the attributes of Tui manifest on the physical plane of your daily life.

Next, think of the number 6.

This is another important corner of the hall since it is the corner of the patriarch, and represents the leader, the king, the commander who brings wealth and gold into your home. Here too is the place where heaven luck is channelled into your home bringing with it all manner of good fortune related to helpful people, mentors and powerful friends. The trigram of this sector is the powerful Chien, made up of three solid unbroken yang lines. It is therefore the most yang corner of your hall. The direction here is north-west and the element is big metal or big gold. Visualize a mountain of gold in this corner of your hall. Watch the gold shimmer and glitter in this corner, creating magnificent heaven-sent luck into your hall and your home. Visualize this mountain of gold very strongly. Keep telling yourself that this is the north-west corner of your Hall of Eight Aspirations.

Next, think of the number 1.

This sector corresponds to the north sector of your mentally created hall. Remind yourself that you are in the Hall of Eight Aspirations which is located in your perfect home. Look at the compass on the floor and see where the north is. Once you have your orientation, move into the corner that corresponds to the north. Think strongly that you are standing in the north sector and here the wall has been painted blue to reflect the water element. And in this corner there is a beautiful koi pond. This is the place of water and its gentle gurgling presence here in a fishpond activates powerful career luck for you. The trigram is Kan, which symbolizes water. Here all you need to do is concentrate on the water bringing you lots of career luck. Do this visualization when you are in line for promotion or when you are eyeing a particular job. Anyone who wants to climb the corporate career ladder will benefit from this visualization. Picture the pond as very clean and the fish inside as being very happy. Fish are wonderful symbols of abundance. You may visualize the dragon fish, also known as the arrowana; or beautiful deeply coloured red goldfish. Or picture a school of tetras, angelfish or guppies swimming happily in the clean water, energizing your career luck for you. Do this visualization regularly if you want to go far in your career.

Next, think of the number 8.

This is an extremely lucky number which corresponds to the direction north-east and the element of earth. This is the literary corner that benefits scholars and those engaged in a programme of study, meditation and retreat. It can also be considered the wisdom corner, excellent for doing meditations. In the Hall of Eight Aspirations the north-east corner signifies a mountain holding still, in preparation for a wealth of good things about to happen.

So visualize a mountain in this corner, and imagine that inside this mountain is plenty of precious treasure. Get mental help by picturing the trigram Ken which stands for mountain and is made up of an unbroken yang line above two broken yin lines. Thinking of this trigram evokes strengthening chi, which benefits the mind greatly. So one benefit of this visualization is that it will speed up your development as a practitioner of meditation, visualization and inner feng shui.

From 8 we move on to the number 3.

We have reached the wood sector of the hall. The direction is east and the trigram here is Chen signified by two broken yin lines sitting on one solid yang line. The season is spring. This corner of the hall signifies new beginnings. It is the corner which governs the health of residents. Healthy growing plants here will cause there to be good health at home. Faded, dried or dying plants will cause all kinds of health problems to surface. So visualize this corner as a profusion of plants and flowers growing lush and happy. This is like your indoor garden patch and the better the plants grow the more auspicious and upward-reaching will be the chi energy created. Visualize very strongly.

And finally think of the number 4.

This is the corner of south-east, the sector that governs the luck of wealth. Here the trigram is Sun, which is the image of the wind signified by a single broken line below two solid yang lines. Picture the wind scattering seeds to all the corners of the world. The seeds fall to the ground, penetrate the soil and take root. Soon they begin to germinate and a plant grows. It blooms, flowers and produces more seeds, which are once again scattered by the wind. The cycle of prosperity is never ending. Thus does this image create wealth over and over again. Picture this cycle of wealth creation strongly and mentally energize the corner with water and plants.

When you have mentally walked through your Hall of Eight Aspirations once you may wish to survey the hall again before leaving it… Think of it as bright and filled with sunlight in the daytime and moonlight at night. The Hall of Eight Aspirations is completely under your control. You can transform it in any way you wish, and depending on which of the eight aspirations is important to you, you can spend time doing more work in the corners and sectors that matter the most.

The garden of your perfect home

Take your time moving from one part of your perfect home to another. Look around you. See the flowers and plants and trees in your garden. Smell the scents and breathe in the clean fresh air. Create magic with your mind as you plan the colours of the flowers and the types of plants you place in different parts of the garden.

Create auspicious water features in your garden. Place pretty ponds and cascading waterfalls filled with abundant fishes in the north, east and south-east of your garden. Plant tall trees behind your home and create an orchard of fruit trees in the eastern part of the garden. Plant a clump of bamboo in the west. When you create flowerbeds, make them meander along the edges of your garden so they resemble the celestial dragon. The same too of little streams and rivers. Let these meander and let all water features seem to 'bring water towards the home'. Do not let rivers flow away from the home; always towards the home.

The rooms of your perfect home

Look at the rooms in your paradise home and let your creativity flow. Decorate them as you wish and place windchimes, lights, mirrors and good fortune symbols in a way that conforms to what you know of feng shui. Arrange your chairs and beds, tables and cabinets so that they do not block the flow of chi. Place them so that you always face in your best directions.

Look above at all your ceilings. Note that they are free of heavy structural beams or big pieces of wood. There are no pillars and protruding corners either. In your perfect home there are no poison arrows camouflaged to do you harm.

Your perfect home is an ideal place for feng shui practice. Here you engage your inner mind consciousness to assist you to enhance your knowledge of feng shui on the physical level. Sharpen your awareness of harmony and balance. Tune into the vibrations and energy of the cosmos. Immerse yourself in a profusion of hues and colours and feel the moods which these colours invoke in you. Vary the intensity of colours and lights and tune into them. You will develop an instinct for the colours that are particularly good for you.

Anything that displeases you in your perfect home can be dissolved in a split second simply with your thoughts. Anything can appear or disappear. Get used to thinking this way. Your home is your palace. It must be comfortable for you. It must feel safe and secure. It must be a sanctuary. Sit in your perfect home savouring its radiance and charm and peace. Absorb the ambience which you have created in your mind.

When you do this visualization regularly, your perfect home will eventually materialize before your very eyes. It will happen without you realizing it. This is what is meant when we describe 'dream homes'. The mind creates a perfect feng shui home when you undertake this extended visualization exercise in conjunction with the study of feng shui. The process of understanding feng shui then takes place at two levels of consciousness: at the surface level as well as at the inner subconscious level. Your practice of feng shui then becomes extremely powerful.

Contacting the inner feng shui guide

When you have been studying and reading about feng shui for a while you will begin to feel that you want to discuss it with someone sympathetic and perhaps go deeper. Practising feng shui is not very difficult. But it requires you to be rather disciplined in your study, very focused in your motivations and most of all very confident in your practice. When you are honest and genuine in your desire to learn you will attract genuine feng shui masters into your life. There is also, deep within each one of us, an inner guide who knows all about living in harmony with the chi of one's environment. This inner guide personifies the deep intuitive wisdom inside all of us.

To make contact with this inner feng shui guide, use the excellent visualization given on p. 178. The starting point is the desire to make contact. If you consciously wish to connect with your own inner and higher wisdom, then you are ready to do so. It is important to acknowledge from the start that this guide is a product of your imagination. He or she is made real by the power of your own mind. He or she is the wisdom and strength that resides inside you.

Think for a few moments about this. The inner feng shui guide is not a ghost, a spirit, an angel, a wise man or any of these fancy images. But if it makes you happier to think of the inner guide in any of these ways, that too is fine. Your inner guide can take any form, but usually his/her manifestation will conform to your inner view of a trusted, wise and knowing person. So keep an open mind when you undertake this visualization.

Meeting with the inner guide is exceptionally rewarding for those serious about wanting to use feng shui to enhance their lives. I cannot even begin to tell you how often I 'speak' with my inner feng shui guides and masters (yes, in the plural). I have different guides for different schools of feng shui, and we have lengthy discussions about the practical side of many feng shui theories. Sometimes we have 'meetings': this happens when I am undecided about a certain feng shui interpretation, or when I am unsure about the authenticity of something passed on to me by a feng shui practitioner.

My attitude towards the study and practice of feng shui is simple and straightforward: unless a feng shui guideline is something I have seen work, either for myself or for someone else, and unless the recommendation makes sense, I will not consider it authentic. So I always discuss new feng shui knowledge with my own inner guides.

Everyone knows a little bit about feng shui from their previous existences, i.e. their past lives. Where feng shui practice may go wrong is in the application and interpretation. This happens when there is insufficient experience or when knowledge is wholly inadequate. I discuss with my own inner guides because I believe they have a history of practising feng shui which goes back many centuries.

As a beginner it is a good idea to work with an inner feng shui guide or several guides who will play the role(s) of devil's advocate, confidant, master and colleague in your study. Start connecting with one guide and let him/her bring you future guides when you are ready.

So let us start ...

Relax and breathe deeply.

When you have reached a good rhythm of breathing visualize yourself in your perfect home. Take your time going to your home, which exists in the alpha levels of your mind consciousness. Be very relaxed.

Now visualize yourself taking a walk down a path that winds itself round the hills near your home.

The path seems to go on for ever but you feel very safe. In the distance you see high mountains and beyond that the distant horizon. Fill yourself with expectations that you will soon meet your inner feng shui guide.

Soon you come to a clearing where the path widens. The distant horizon becomes clearer. Now as you gaze into the horizon, without forcing yourself, let the image of a bright and clear light manifest itself in the distance. This light moves towards you and as it gets nearer it takes the shape and form of a person.

At first the image is hazy but as you feel yourself reaching out towards the apparition the features become clearer. You recognize him/her immediately as your memory takes a strong jolt. Here is someone you have known inside your head for as long as you can remember. You feel a surge of affinity emanating between you. There is instant rapport as you stare at each other. The smiles are broad and the mood is happy, expectant.

Spend the next few minutes just soaking in the guide's appearance. There is no need to rush into immediate conversation. Sometimes the first meeting is simply soaking up each other's presence. You can sit on a nearby rock. You may shake hands or exchange pleasantries. Do what comes naturally. Don't worry what your inner guide looks like. He/she can take any shape, be any person, speak any language. He can be a feng shui master you are studying with, or your own best friend. He can be the author of the book you are reading at the time. Whoever your inner guide turns out to be, there must be immediate affinity, a feeling of trust and good will.

Later when you start communicating with your inner guide, you can ask questions: who he is, his relationship with you (if any) in the past. Where he learned his feng shui. Where he is from, and so forth. Let answers flow freely from your mind to his. In the early days, conversation may seem stilted and difficult but after some time your feeling of affinity will grow.

Sometimes your guide will ask you questions. Conversation is a two-way flow. Request your guide to tell you if there is anything she feels you ought to know or concentrate on. Ask her for any advice. If you wish, you can take your inner guide into your confidence about specific problems.

Do not expect immediate answers. Always allow time for your guide to develop closeness. Make sure you understand the main points of answers given. When you feel that your meeting is complete, say goodbye and make another date to meet. Then slowly walk back home and as you walk, surface back into the realm of physical existence.

Different people will develop their inner guide meetings in different ways; this guided visualization is only to get you started. What we are indulging in here can be described as an esoteric exercise. It is a metaphysical experience which grows more 'normal' as the weeks progress. Eventually you will find that you accept the esoteric as normal and the metaphysical as the natural state of being.

Inner feng shui visualization is a very private practice. You should not feel it necessary to share your innermost secrets and thoughts with anyone else, and in fact I advise against it. You do not require help from another person. The exercise does not grow 'stronger' with more 'energy' from more people. It is not masses of energy we are looking for. Success is not enhanced by quantity. Success is enhanced by *focused* energy. The more concentrated you are, the sharper will be the power of your inner mind consciousness.

If you want more company, ask your inner guide to bring more feng shui experts from another realm to aid you. But refrain from allowing another person to do joint visualizations with you. It does not help and it might be harmful.

Tapping the energy of the cosmos

A visualization which is a great favourite of mine fills the body, mind and spirit with the energies of the cosmos. Here you have to use your imagination to create pathways for the energies of earth and sky to flow harmoniously through your body. This exercise will get the chi inside your body and mind to flow harmoniously and in rhythm with the cosmos.

Earth energy is useful in keeping you 'grounded' i.e. keeping you stable, firm and grounded in the physical plane of reality. It ensures that you never get 'spaced out' during your visualization exercises, which take you deep into the inner realms of your mind.

Sky energy taps into the energy fields of the cosmos, enabling you to access the energies of vision, fantasy, imagination and creativity. Sky energy is light and floating. When you are filled with sky energy it helps you to transcend into a plane of lightness where gravity is non-existent and where you float lightly and gently, sometimes rising high above the clouds and even visiting the pure worlds of other realms. Sky energy sometimes takes you into other worlds and other dimensions of existence, so don't be afraid when you feel you are floating. Don't resist. Just go with the flow.

Tapping these two sources of energy at the same time creates a beautiful balance inside your mind and body. It increases your sense of well-being and expands your powers of manifestation. It also heightens your awareness of the realms of fantasy yet connects you with the reality of your physical existence. So let us begin...

Sit quietly in your meditation room. Keep your back straight.

Make sure you are very comfortable and then start to breathe deeply. Gently lower your eyes as you follow your breath.

When you have attained a comfortable rhythm in your breathing imagine yourself going down deep into your alpha level of consciousness. Feel your brain waves slowing down.

You are deep down in your alpha level now.

Now visualize a long cord about two inches in diameter attached to the base of your spine and extending down through the floor and into the earth. The cord is going down very deep into the earth. Think of this cord as your rooting cord.

Spend a few moments feeling the warm, grounding earth energy rising from the earth and entering your body as the precious earth chi. This earth chi is filled with magic of the earth and it keeps you firmly centred and grounded. In appearance it looks like a dark yellow light similar to the colour of saffron water. Feel the energy of the earth as warm, comforting and protective. Feel it flowing up through the cord; up through your spine into your body, and into your head and then leaving through the top of your head. Keep following this flow of earth energy until you know that the flow is firmly established. You are so firm and so strongly rooted to the earth that you are unshakeable.

Now visualize the energy of the sky. It takes the appearance of bright blue white light and it flows in through the top of your head, entering your body through the crown chakra. It flows down into your seat, and then down through your rooting cord into the depths of the earth. The energy of the sky has a completely different feeling from earth energy. Where earth energy is warm and grounding, sky energy is light and soaring. It makes you feel as if you can fly. It is cool and enlightening. Sky energy makes you connect with your heaven luck.

When you have established the two kinds of energies flowing smoothly through your mind and body, feel them mixing harmoniously. The energies do not mix like coloured water dissolving into each other. They are two sets of lights merging. Neither overcomes the other. Both energies are transparent with neither substance nor form. You feel the energy flow from top to bottom and into the earth, and from bottom to top before flowing out into the cosmos.

This visualization is an excellent exercise either to start or to close your sessions each day. Stay for a while with the image of the energies flowing through your body. Feel your body and mind becoming strongly charged, and then slowly come out of meditation by opening your eyes. You should feel your mind becoming clear and focused.

Unlocking the chakras or energy zones

Unlocking the seven energy zones within your physical body is an exquisite way of keeping the energy inside you flowing smoothly. It is an exercise that refreshes and makes you mentally alert.

The energy zones of the body are centred around your 'chakras', the vital power points of your body. (See p. 111 for a diagram of your chakra centres. Chakra meditation is used to enhance the flow of chi within the body.) The following visualization activates the chakras and it is necessary to put some safeguards into place before you do this visualization.

You do this by creating a halo of light as an invisible shield, which prevents the energies of your chakras from escaping.

Lie down flat on your back with your arms by your sides and your hands resting lightly palm down on your stomach. Close your eyes and breathe deeply and gently. Slowly feel yourself relax. Now gently tighten the muscles of your anus. Continue breathing deeply and gently.

Now visualize a halo of gentle white light surrounding your whole body from the top of your head to the tips of your toes. You are cocooned inside this halo of white light. Be very relaxed.

Imagine a bright glowing ball of golden white light at the top of your head. This is your crown chakra. Breathe deeply in and out eight times, concentrating on the ball of light. Feel it radiate from the top of your head.

Now let your mind move down slowly to your forehead just between your eyes. This is your inner eye chakra which enables you to 'see' things spiritual when it has been sufficiently purified and energized. Imagine a ball of golden white light emanating from the inner eye. Picture the light shining with great brilliance.

Let your concentration move to your throat chakra. Once again the golden white ball of light lights up the throat area as light comes forth from within you. Next move to your heart zone. This is the heart chakra: let the golden ball of white light gather brilliance as it reaches the heart chakra. The brilliant light coming out from the heart chakra illuminates the whole chest area.

Now move to the solar plexus and picture the ball of white light glowing in your stomach area. Then the ball of light illuminates the lower abdominal area and finally it lights up the root chakra in the vicinity of the pelvic area. When all seven zones are glowing and throbbing with golden white light, feel them radiating powerful chi energy. Your body resembles a strand of sparkling diamonds. Hold this vision strongly in your mind, and empower it with strong concentration.

After a few moments, imagine energy flowing from the top of your head down through your body and leaving your body at the root chakra then going up into your head again, repeating the circular flow several times. Maintain this flow of energy for a few minutes. Now begin to close the energy centres. Start at the root chakra and work upwards, visualizing the balls of light moving up, each merging with the one above. When you reach the top of the head visualize the light slowly ascending until it dissolves into the cosmos. Rest for a few minutes before opening your eyes. You will feel very strongly energized.

Chamber of colours

Colour plays a significant part in enhancing the practice of inner feng shui. It is a wonderful tool for feng shui visualization because each of the seven colours – red, orange, yellow, green, blue, lilac and purple – has the power to evoke strong emotional feelings within the human mind. These colour vibrations assist body and mind chi to connect with the chi of the environment.

Some colours evoke a sense of coolness, generating calm and serenity – positive yin feelings that provide a good balance when there is an excess of yang energy. Other colours thrill and excite, speak loudly and inspire: such colours become energizing when there is a lack of yang energy. Each colour has its own affinity energy zone within the body, inspiring certain feelings. Familiarize yourself with these associations and attributes before embarking on the Chamber of Colours visualization.

Red opens the energy zone of the root chakra at the base of the spine. It generates warmth, fire heat, action. It creates a sense of purpose and determination and is powerful in burning away negative mental conditioning. Bathing in a chamber of red light removes all negative thoughts and strengthens the root chakra.

Orange opens the pelvic areas of the body. It builds creative and sexual energies and helps strengthen concentration and give a sense of purpose.

Yellow energizes the stomach area. It represents sunlight, warmth and activity and is particularly powerful in manifesting creative energy on the physical plane. Yellow also lifts depression, producing a sense of well-being and cheerfulness.

Green relaxes and energizes the heart area and cools heated emotion and fevers. It heightens prosperity consciousness, strengthens the physical heart and enhances the ability to accept love. It also generates warm feelings of security and makes you feel at peace with the world.

Blue opens the energy around the throat area. It is calming and soothing and is associated with love. It heals and relaxes. It has the power to open channels to love and wisdom. Blue is a spiritual colour which increases sensitivity and heightens awareness of subtle energies. It is a very powerful.

Lilac symbolizes gentleness, love and peace. It is associated with the heart and mind. Lilac enhances inventiveness and resourcefulness and is especially good at lifting depression and despair. When you are feeling defeated, take a lilac bath. It will do you no end of good.

Purple increases spiritual awareness. It is the premier colour for healing, both physical and mental. It harmonizes with all other colours and it energizes the head's crown chakra. At its peak intensity it becomes white light, which is the amalgamation of all the colours.

There are many ways to work with colours, but I have discovered that the most effective and fastest way to create the colour energies indicated is to 'take a bath' in coloured light. Do this by creating a Chamber of Colours.

Visualize a chamber bathed in any one of the seven colours. Each time you need to activate any of the colours just sit in a meditative posture, close your eyes, breathe deeply, relax and then visualize yourself entering the chamber of lights. Turn the switch according to which colour bath you want, then picture yourself relaxing in the chamber completely bathed in the glow of the colour you feel you need.

To help in the visualization, try physically to stare at each of the colours first before attempting to visualize yourself surrounded by the colour. Coloured light bulbs with their characteristic brilliance can be very helpful. Or you can try staring at pictures that have solid colours. Either way you are educating your mind in the pigments and shades you wish to visualize.

Exercising with colours enhances your powers of visualization to activate inner feng shui using your mind, so create your chamber of colours as frequently as possible. When you do so, immerse yourself completely in each colour in turn, and always end this visualization with white light. This purifies any negative thoughts that have strayed into your consciousness during your meditative session. With the complete dissolution of negativity in your inner mind, the practice of feng shui at every level of consciousness becomes a fun-filled and exhilarating exercise.

Remember, you can do it all yourself. There is no need to delegate your destiny or your well-being to anyone else. You must create your own mankind luck. Educate your mind to this fact and feng shui will reward you with great good fortune far beyond your expectations.

Meet Lillian Too...

Lillian Too was the first woman in Asia to become the Chief Executive Officer of a Bank – the Grindlays Dao Heng Bank in Hong Kong. In Malaysia, where she comes from, Lillian Too is described by *Malaysian Business*, the country's leading business magazine as, '... something of a legend in corporate circles being the first woman there to become the Managing Director of a publicly listed company.'

Lillian is an MBA graduate from the Harvard Business School, in Boston USA. She has also been described as being 'in a league of her own' by one of the country's leading magazines: *Success*. The internationally acclaimed *Vogue* magazine describes her 'as someone people listen to'.

Lillian was not simply a successful corporate woman. As a business lady she also made enough money never to have to work again. In the early Nineties, she retired from working life to become a full-time mother. That was when she started a new career in writing. To date she has penned 28 bestsellers, 26 of which are on her favourite subject of feng shui, which she says was greatly responsible for giving her masses of luck during her corporate career days, and in her business dealings. Her feng shui books have been translated into 19 languages.

In 1997, the phenomenal worldwide success of her internationally published book *The Complete Illustrated Guide to Feng Shui* made waves in the non-fictional book trade. Released in October 1996, the book has made the bestseller lists of various countries, including the UK's Bookwatch list. It also became the number one bestseller over the summer of 1997 in the Barnes and Noble bestseller list of the United States.

Her latest achievement has been the successful launch of her *Feng Shui Kit*, as well as her series of *Feng Shui Fundamentals* – nine little books advising how to use feng shui in nine easy lessons, and how to use feng shui for love, wealth, career, health, children, networking, fame and education In the spring of 1998, Rider books, an imprint of Random House, published *Feng Shui Essentials* with considerable success and followed this in 1999 with *Creating Abundance*. Lillian Too is married and has one daughter.

Lillian Too's website

Readers may email Lillian Too at feng shui@lillian-too.com. They can also visit www.worldoffengshui.com to get regular updates on time dimension feng shui, the good and bad dates based on the Almanac, plus regular features on tips, the fine points of feng shui practice, questions and answers to and from Aunt Agga, and loads more. This has now become the most extensive website online magazine on the subject of feng shui. Many of the regular columns are updated as frequently as fortnightly and monthly ...

If you would like to order any of the following or to receive our catalogue please fill in the form below:

Lillian Too's Essential Feng Shui	£12.99
Creating Abundance by Lillian Too	£12.99
How To Make Your First Million by Lillian Too	£4.99
Interior Design with Feng Shui by Sarah Rossbach	£6.99
Feng Shui by Sarah Rossbach	£6.99
Feng Shui Step by Step by T. Raphael Simons	£12.99
The Ki by Takashi Yoshikawa	£12.99
Sacred Space by Denise Linn	£6.99

HOW TO ORDER

BY POST: TBS Direct, TBS Ltd, Colchester Road, Frating Green, Essex CO7 7DW

Please send me _____ copies of_____

_____@ £ _____ each

☐ I enclose my cheque for £ _____ payable to Rider Books

☐ Please charge £ _____ to my American Express/Visa/Mastercard account*
   (*delete as applicable)

Card No ☐☐☐☐☐☐☐☐☐☐☐☐☐☐☐☐☐☐

Expiry Date: ☐☐☐☐   Signature _____

Name _____

Address _____

_____ Postcode _____

Delivery address if different _____

_____ Postcode _____

Or call our credit card hotline on 01206 255800.

Please have your card details handy.

Please quote reference: InnerFeng

Rider is an imprint of Random House UK Ltd